改訂版

やっておきたい 英語長文 500

［問題編］

河合塾講師

杉山 俊一
塚越 友幸
山下 博子
［共著］

河合出版

河合塾
SERIES

改訂版

やってきたい 英語長文 500

[問題編]

河合塾講師

杉山 俊一
塚越 友幸
山下 博子
[共著]

河合出版

1

25 min.
454 words

次の英文を読んで，設問に答えなさい。

Listening to a gardening program the other day, I was struck by something the expert said about a particular type of potted plant. Do not water it once it has *come into bud, he advised. Cause it to feel stress, and it will produce more, and more beautiful, flowers.

Surely (1)this advice is against everything that we are told by doctors. Stress is bad for us, they say. Stress is the cause of all sorts of diseases. Stress caused by overwork sometimes results in early death. Newspaper and magazine articles tell us how to reduce stress, or how to avoid it altogether. No one has a good word for stress.

And yet, I asked myself, if stress is good for plants, can there possibly be any value for us in it? (2)The longer I thought about it, the more it seemed to me that there is. Without a certain degree of tension and stress, we are apt to become lazy and neglect our duties. All students know that they should study regularly throughout the year, and then be able to face examinations without fear. In fact, most students leave this study till the last possible moment, and then hastily try to (3) lost time.

Many of us, likewise, put off dealing with our problems until the deadline approaches. Every year I resolve that I will write all my Christmas cards and letters ahead of time, and avoid a last-minute rush; and every year I find that once again I have left it too late for me to finish comfortably. Only when the tension increases (4)[working seriously / the job / do / to get / I / done / start].

In other fields too, when satisfaction enters in, creativity and curiosity go out of the window. What has been called (5)"divine discontent" — a creative dissatisfaction with the present situation, whatever it is — produces progress. And that dissatisfaction is one type of stress.

Thus, it seemed to me, a certain degree of stress is necessary for human progress. Just how much is good, and how much is harmful, is the problem.

(6)Those of us who are employed by a company whose policies demand long periods of stressful activity are to be sympathized with, since too much stress is counterproductive. Those of us who are self-employed may have more freedom to choose our own best level of stress. In either case, we need some preparation before the period of stress in order to be able to succeed.

So, like the potted plant in question, if we are watered sufficiently to begin with, and then left to struggle for a while on our own, we too may produce more and better flowers than one who, over-protected, has never had to try.

（注） come into bud：(木などが)芽を出す

(龍谷大)

問1 下線部(1)の内容として最も適当なものを，次のア～エから１つ選びなさい。

ア．植物に水をやりすぎてはいけない。

イ．医者から言われたことは必ず守る。

ウ．できるだけストレスを感じないようにする。

エ．美しい花を多く咲かせるために植物にストレスを与える。

問2 下線部(2)を省略された部分の意味を明らかにして日本語に訳しなさい。

問3 空所(　3　)に入れるのに最も適当なものを，次のア～エから１つ選びなさい。

ア．do away with　イ．make up for　ウ．put up with　エ．run out of

問4 下線部(4)の語(句)を文意が通るように並べ換えなさい。

問5 下線部(5)の内容として最も適当なものを，次のア～エから１つ選びなさい。

ア．mental sickness　イ．indifference to stress

ウ．a complaint against morality　エ．a desire for improvement

問6 下線部(6)を日本語に訳しなさい。

問7 本文の内容と一致するものを，次のア～エから１つ選びなさい。

ア．ストレスがなければのびのびといい仕事ができる。

イ．ある種のストレスは創造力や好奇心をかきたてる。

ウ．鉢植えの植物はかかさず水をやればたくさん花が咲く。

エ．現状に対する不満は大きなストレスを生み，それが人に悪い影響を及ぼす。

2

35 min.
545 words

次の英文を読んで，設問に答えなさい。

In 1800, a *stuffed animal arrived in England from the newly discovered continent of Australia. The continent had already been the source of plants and animals never seen before — but this one was ridiculous. It was nearly two feet long, and had fur-covered skin. It also had a flat rubber-like bill, a piece of skin between its toes, a broad flat tail, and a *spur on each hind leg that was clearly intended to produce poison. What's more, under the tail was a single opening.

Zoologists stared at the thing in disbelief. Hair like a mammal! Bill and feet like an aquatic or water bird! Poison spurs like a snake! A single opening in the rear as though it laid eggs!

There was an explosion of anger. The thing was a joke. (1)Some unfunny joker in Australia, taking advantage of the distance and strangeness of the continent, had stitched together parts of widely different creatures and was intent on making fools of innocent zoologists in England.

Yet the skin seemed to fit together. There were no signs of artificial joining. Was it or was it not a fake? And if it wasn't a fake, (2)was it a mammal with reptilian characteristics, or a reptile with mammalian characteristics, or was it partly bird, or what?

The discussion went on heatedly for decades. Even the name emphasized the ways in which it didn't seem like a mammal despite its hair. One early name was *Platypus anatinus*, which is Latin for "Flat-foot, duck-like." Unfortunately, the term "platypus" had already been applied to a type of beetle and there could be no duplication in scientific names. It therefore received another name, *Ornithorhynchus paradoxus*, which means "Bird-beak, paradoxical."

Slowly, however, zoologists had to reach agreement and admit that the creature was real and not a fake, however upsetting it might be to zoological notions. For one thing, there were increasingly reliable reports from people in Australia who caught glimpses of the creature alive. The *paradoxus* was dropped and the scientific name is now *Ornithorhynchus anatinus*.

To the general public, however, it is the "*duckbill platypus," or even just the duckbill, the queerest mammal (assuming it is a mammal) in the world.

(3)When specimens were received in such condition as to make it possible to study the internal organs, it appeared that the heart was just like those of mammals and not at all like those of reptiles. The egg-forming machinery in the female, however, was not at all like that of mammals, but like that of birds or reptiles. It seemed really and truly to be an egg-layer.

It wasn't till 1884, however, that the actual eggs laid by a creature with hair were found. They were not the eggs of a platypus, but another Australian species, the *spiny anteater. That was worth an excited announcement. A group of British scientists were meeting in Montreal at the time, and the egg-discoverer, W. H. Caldwell, sent them a message to announce the finding.

It wasn't till the twentieth century that the intimate life of the duckbill came to be known. It is an aquatic animal, living in Australian fresh water at a wide variety of temperatures — from tropical streams at sea level to cold lakes at an elevation of a mile.

（注） stuffed：剥製の　　spur：かぎづめ　　duckbill platypus：カモノハシ
spiny anteater：ハリモグラ

（東北大）

問1　下線部(1)を日本語に訳しなさい。

問2　英国の動物学者たちが下線部(2)のような疑問を抱いた理由を，本文に即して70字以内の日本語で述べなさい。

問3　下線部(3)を日本語に訳しなさい。

問4　カモノハシの学名が *Platypus anatinus* から *Ornithorhynchus paradoxus* に変更された理由を簡潔に日本語で述べなさい。

問5　本文の内容と一致するものを，次のア～クから３つ選びなさい。

ア．Plants and animals brought from Australia were all familiar and the duckbill was no exception.

イ．By the end of the nineteenth century, zoologists already understood the life of duckbills completely.

ウ．What had seemed like egg-forming machinery turned out to be an organ for swimming.

エ．It was discovered that there are creatures other than duckbills that lay eggs though they are mammals.

オ. We now know that duckbills can only live in a limited range of water temperatures.

カ. When the first duckbill was introduced, some people were angry, some considered it artificial, and some stared at it in disbelief.

キ. Zoologists kept on discussing heatedly for decades where the stuffed animal had come from.

ク. A message informed British scientists in Montreal of the existence of eggs laid by a creature with hair, other than the duckbill.

3

30 min.
423 words

次の英文を読んで，設問に答えなさい。

Handwriting is a valuable diagnostic tool. It gives a measurable and permanent indication of the writer's stage of development, and sometimes their state of mind, at any particular moment. Our own handwriting, for instance, may change when we are tired or tense. (1)It may alter depending on whether we like the person we are writing to or not. However, there would be more fundamental differences to our usual writing if real problems were involved. Supposing we had an accident and had to learn to write with our non-preferred hand; supposing we developed an illness that left us with a tremor; or supposing we suffered a nervous breakdown, would we expect our handwriting to remain unchanged? (2), so we should realize that the writing of children who may be suffering from any of a wide variety of conditions will reflect these conditions. In the classroom they are often expected to be able to attain the same level of handwriting as pupils with no similar problems. If we could look at handwriting problems as an indicator and a diagnostic tool instead of measuring problem handwriting against some mythical norm, this would be a positive and major step forward.

(3)Schools may be accustomed to accepting that children termed 'clumsy' may never excel at gymnastics or games, even after the therapy that such children deserve to receive. If these children's motor co-ordination is such that they find difficulty, for example, in catching a ball, then this awkwardness will quite likely be reflected in their handwriting. They may never be able to produce the neat, conventional handwriting that some teachers expect. Awkward hands are likely to produce awkward handwriting, so children should not be scolded (4)[have / conditions / they / over / for / little / which] control. If they are repeatedly criticized for producing 'untidy' written work, then tension will be added to their natural clumsiness. (5)This will only make the situation worse. Of course, any practical advice that might assist the writer, especially in the way of changes in writing posture, should be given. Apart from that, providing the handwriting is (6) enough for the writer to keep up in class, surely those children deserve praise for the way they are tackling a job that is more difficult for them than for others. A positive attitude is most likely to relax the writer. This relaxation will probably be reflected in their written work, and any resulting praise will help to improve the self-image of these children who daily have to see their best efforts condemned as untidy.

(信州大)

問1　下線部(1)を It の内容を明らかにして日本語に訳しなさい。

問2　空所(　2　)に入れるのに最も適当なものを，次のア～エから1つ選びなさい。

ア．It depends　　イ．That's what happens

ウ．Of course not　　エ．It certainly is

問3　下線部(3)を日本語に訳しなさい。

問4　下線部(4)の語を文意が通るように並べ換えなさい。

問5　下線部(5)の内容を50字以内の日本語で述べなさい。

問6　空所(　6　)に入れるのに最も適当なものを，次のア～エから1つ選びなさい。

ア．simple but slow　　イ．compact but rational

ウ．legible and fast　　エ．complex and elaborate

問7　英文のタイトルとして最も適当なものを，次のア～エから1つ選びなさい。

ア．Good handwriting leads to success

イ．Handwriting tells a lot about a writer

ウ．How to improve your handwriting

エ．The writing of children

4

30 min.
465 words

次の英文を読んで，設問に答えなさい。

It's interesting how much e-mail affects our personal space. While some businesses have replaced much inter-office phone communication with e-mail, most users see e-mail as a medium that protects their private space far more than the telephone. E-mail gives us the freedom to communicate (1)<u>on our own terms</u>: it's possible for us to communicate without allowing anyone to hear our voice or see our face.

While e-mail offers personal privacy, it also enables us to start a conversation with people we aren't acquainted with. We send e-mail to people we would rarely telephone or request to see face-to-face. Of course, the people we send messages to have the option to respond at their own convenience — or not at all. (2)<u>There is a growing tendency to make e-mail addresses, but not phone numbers, public</u>. This practice is a result of the increasing acceptance of e-mail as a form of direct contact, even with well-known people we usually couldn't approach in person.

If there is no voice to hear and no face to see, many e-mail users become very open about the information they are willing to reveal on-line. (3)<u>The lack of visual and auditory signals greatly increases the amount of information speakers are willing to let others know about themselves</u>. People write things in e-mails they would not want to say in a face-to-face conversation or on the telephone.

An important point is the degree of exposure a person perceives. Investigators in one study demonstrated that even (4) reduces your sense of privacy. In the experiment, participants were asked to comment either on intimate or on non-intimate topics while sitting alone in one of two small rooms and speaking into a microphone. One room had bare walls; the other contained a large mirror. When discussing intimate topics, participants in the mirrored room were less likely to enjoy the task, had the longest times before answering questions, gave the shortest answers, and gave less intimate information than those who couldn't see themselves. Thus, the more we keep our personal details private, the more likely we are to speak our minds.

(5)E-mail as we know it allows a high degree of privacy, which, in turn, helps generate more openness. There are continuing reports from parents about e-mail communication with their children who have left home for college. Sons and daughters who had little to say to their parents while still in high school, who even now rarely write or phone home, commonly e-mail just to "chat."

Similarly, research on the role of computers has shown that people offer more (6) information about themselves when answering questions using a computer than when answering the same questions on paper or through a face-to-face interview. The differences were especially noticeable when the information at issue was personally sensitive.

(愛知県立大)

問1 下線部(1)とほぼ同じ意味を表すものを，次のア～エから１つ選びなさい。

ア．in the interests of others　　イ．the way we want others to

ウ．in our own words　　エ．the way we want to

問2 下線部(2)の理由を30字程度の日本語で述べなさい。

問3 下線部(3)を日本語に訳しなさい。

問4 空所(4)に入れるのに最も適当なものを，次のア～エから１つ選びなさい。

ア．seeing yourself　　イ．hearing yourself

ウ．seeing others　　エ．hearing others

問5 下線部(5)を日本語に訳しなさい。

問6 空所(6)に入れるのに最も適当なものを，次のア～エから１つ選びなさい。

ア．incorrect and biased　　イ．accurate and complete

ウ．official and recent　　エ．general and interesting

5

30 min.
507 words

次の英文を読んで，設問に答えなさい。

Until recently, Kovalam, a small fishing village in India's Kerala state, could not keep up with its rising popularity. (1)Attracted by clean beaches, friendly people and a relaxed way of life, visitors from as far away as Europe began coming in large numbers to the region in the mid-1960s. Over the next two decades, investors rushed in to meet the demand, building row upon row of new hotels, restaurants and souvenir shops. But in 1993 the tourist stream began to slow. By 2000, the number of tourists had decreased by 40 percent.

Travel experts (2a)ruled out economic factors and shifting tourist tastes, finally explaining the decline as one caused by the community's waste management problems. Like many popular destinations in the developing world, Kovalam has no formal plan to deal with the growing levels of garbage generated by tourists. Hotels and other facilities collect recyclable items, such as glass, paper and metal scraps, for reuse by local industries whenever possible. The less desirable items — plastic bottles and even uneaten food, for example — simply pile up in towering mounds or are dumped into nearby streams, posing the risk of serious disease.

Yet, a local politician complained, "Nobody bothers about the health issues faced by people. Everybody wants Kovalam beach to be clean just so it can get more business."

These problems are not unique to Kovalam. Increasingly, developing countries are turning to tourism as a way to (2b)diversify their economies, stimulate investments and create earnings.

Tourism is one of the world's least regulated industries. (3)This has implications for communities and cultures around the world. Hotels, tourist transport and related activities consume huge amounts of energy, water and other resources; and they produce pollution, often in destinations that are unprepared to deal with these impacts. In addition, many communities face cultural troubles and other unwelcome changes that accompany higher visitor numbers. (4)Fears of terrorism and the safety of air travel may have lessened interest in some international travel for the time being. However, over the long term the demand for tourism is expected to resume its steady rise.

Many governments, industry groups and others are promoting responsible travel that makes money and creates jobs while also protecting the local environments and cultures. While it does succeed in some circumstances, this kind of environmentally responsible tourism can produce many of the same problems as ordinary tourism, including the creation of waste. In some cases it is little more than a marketing tool for businesses hoping to promote (2c)an environmentally conscious image.

As tourism's impacts, both good and bad, continue to spread, it is more and more important to redirect activities onto a path that protects local resources to the fullest. (5)This will require deep changes that reach far beyond the scope of responsible tourism. A broad range of people and organizations, including executives at large companies, governments, nongovernmental groups and the tourists themselves, will need to become involved with the efforts to protect and maintain, at all levels, the environment and culture of the various places to which tourists go.

（東工大）

問1　下線部(1)を日本語に訳しなさい。

問2　下線部(2a)～(2c)とほぼ同じ意味を表すものを，次のア～エからそれぞれ１つずつ選びなさい。

(2a)
ア．claimed that economic factors and shifting tastes were the main causes
イ．denied that economic factors and shifting tastes were to blame
ウ．found out that economic factors and waste managements violated the laws
エ．found out that tourists tended to choose inexpensive and better tasting food

(2b)
ア．concentrate on a few key areas
イ．produce a range of various products and services
ウ．start trading with many different countries
エ．strictly control their economic output

(2c) ア. an image of a company particularly interested in environmental issues

イ. an image of a company set up in a certain environment

ウ. an image of consumers harming the environment

エ. an image of consumers who know what they want to buy

問3 下線部(3)の内容を30字以内の日本語で述べなさい。

問4 下線部(4)を日本語に訳しなさい。

問5 下線部(5)の内容を日本語で述べなさい。

6

30 min.
499 words

次の英文を読んで，設問に答えなさい。

How often do we say “Of course I believe it — I saw it with my own eyes!” But (1) can we really be so sure what it is that our eyes tell us? For example, take the simple question, “How big is the moon?”

Could any of us make a good estimate of the moon’s size (2) [had / read / astronomers / not / if / what / us / we / tell] about its diameter? What does looking at the moon, or any other object, tell us about its real size? What do we mean by “real” size or “real” shape, or other appearance, for that matter? Can we believe what we see of things; or rather, putting it the other way round, what do we mean when we say we believe that a thing has a certain size or shape?

The brain interprets the image on the *retina in the light of all sorts of other “information” it receives. Perception, in fact, is by no means a simple recording of the details of the world seen outside. It is a selection of those features with which we are familiar. (3) What it amounts to is that we do not so much believe what we see as see what we believe. Seeing is an activity not only of our eyes but of the (4), which works as a sort of selecting machine. Out of all the images presented to it, it chooses for recognition (5) those that fit most closely with the world learned by past experience.

(6) I want to give a few more examples to show how what the brain has learned influences the process we call “seeing things.” Seeing, they say, is believing. But is it? An arrangement can be made in such a way that a person looks through a peephole into a bare corridor, so bare that it gives no clues about distance. If you now show him a piece of white paper in the corridor and ask how large it is, his reply will be influenced by any suggestion you make as to what the piece of paper may be. If you tell him that the particular piece of paper is a business card, he will say that it is quite (7a). Show him the piece of paper at the same distance and tell him that it is a large envelope, and he will say that it is (7b). On the other hand, if you show a very (7c) playing card, say a Queen of Spades, he will say that it is very close, and if you

show a (7d) one he will say it is a long way away, because, you see, playing cards are nearly always of a standard size. In fact, the size of things we perceive depends upon what we otherwise know about them. When we see a car from far away, its image on the retina is no bigger than that of a toy seen near, but we take the surroundings into consideration and give its proper (8).

(注) retina：網膜

(神戸大)

問1 下線部(1)を日本語に訳しなさい。

問2 下線部(2)の語を文意が通るように並べ換えなさい。

問3 下線部(3)を日本語に訳しなさい。

問4 空所(4)に入れるのに最も適当な1語を本文中から探して答えなさい。

問5 下線部(5)を2語で具体的に書き換えなさい。

問6 下線部(6)を日本語に訳しなさい。

問7 空所(7a)～(7d)に入れるのに最も適当なものを，次のア～エからそれぞれ1つずつ選びなさい。

ア．large　　イ．tiny　　ウ．near　　エ．further away

問8 空所(8)に入れるのに最も適当な1語を本文中から探して答えなさい。

7

35 min.
579 words

次の英文を読んで，設問に答えなさい。

We have all had moments when we would have liked to switch on the sunshine or switch off the rain, or to affect the outdoor temperature. Ever since early humans set up home in the nearest cave, or lit the first fire, we have tried to adjust the climate surrounding us — you could call these the first attempts at weather control. Today, weather control might be thought of as a fantasy world for crazy scientists, but there are some kinds of (1)<u>weather modification</u> — though few in number — which are routine in certain areas of human activity.

There is one powerful reason to seek to alter the weather, and that is to reduce the losses, both human and economic, caused by a natural hazard or disaster. There are other reasons but these do not have the same moral force: they may include a desire for economic or even military advantage over a neighbor. Saving human lives and property can be achieved either by modifying the hazard itself or by reducing its impact. These two methods need not be mutually exclusive, and in certain cases (2)<u>a combination</u> may provide the best results. Insurance may also help to soften the blow of damaged property or loss of earnings.

Weather disasters are generally more difficult to control than terrible events such as landslides where large-scale engineering projects can reduce the frequency and the magnitude of the hazard. The destructive forces of the atmosphere, however, far exceed how much control human beings have over them. To illustrate this we can make a rough estimate that a typical winter storm over the Atlantic or Pacific (3)<u>[100,000 / about / as / as / did / energy / much / releases / times]</u> the first atomic bomb. Even if we wanted to interfere with the atmosphere on this scale, the analysis of costs versus benefits would soon see the project cancelled. There are, though, certain circumstances when intervention can work: when the atmosphere is finely balanced between two contrasting states, we can successfully change that balance with relatively little cost and effort. Thus cloud-seeding operations to create rain will never work (4) favorable conditions for the development of clouds, but they may succeed if deep cloud development is already occurring.

(5)Weather modification projects, whether successful or not, bring a variety of problems which make the prospect of large-scale activity in this field very uncertain. Most of the chemicals used in seeding cause pollution, and the disadvantages of these may exceed the advantages achieved by the seeding process. The release of large amounts of heat energy to reduce fog or clouds, or the generation of extensive electric fields to weaken storms may fall into (6)a similar category. But most problematic of all is our inability to restrict the modification effect to the area for which it was intended. For instance, suppressing a *hailstorm over a region of farmland might move the storm activity to a neighboring urban area; the crops would be saved, but in the city, windows would be smashed, motorcars damaged, and people seriously injured. One scarcely dares to imagine the legal consequences of such an event.

(7) We know that hurricanes and typhoons are one of the principal mechanisms that transfer heat energy received from the sun in tropical areas to middle and high *latitudes. If that mechanism were interfered with, who knows what sort of chain reaction might follow? What kind of major climatic changes might turn up in different parts of the world during subsequent months?

(注) hailstorm：あられを伴う嵐　　latitude：緯度

(筑波大)

問1　下線部(1)が行われる理由を60字以内の日本語で答えなさい。

問2　下線部(2)の内容を35字以内の日本語で答えなさい。

問3　下線部(3)の語を文意が通るように並べ換えなさい。

問4　空所(4)に入れるのに最も適当なものを，次のア～エから1つ選びなさい。

ア．on　　イ．out　　ウ．without　　エ．in

問5　下線部(5)を日本語に訳しなさい。

問6　下線部(6)の内容を25字以内の日本語で答えなさい。

問7　空所(7)に入れるのに最も適当なものを，次のア～エから1つ選びなさい。

ア. Nor does it stop there.
イ. Only there does it stop.
ウ. So it is always the case.
エ. Thus it isn’t the case.

8

30 min.
523 words

次の英文を読んで，設問に答えなさい。

There is a large amount of evidence which shows that people believe words to have magic powers. This is most easily illustrated with those very special words, people's names. In the traditions of modern Ethiopia, the real name of a child is (1) to prevent the child from being influenced magically through the use of the name. It is believed that knowledge of the name gives power over the person who bears that name.

Beliefs of this type are widespread throughout the world. In Borneo, for example, (2)<u>the name of a sickly child is traditionally changed so that the spirits tormenting it will be deceived and leave the child alone</u>. The spirits, apparently, can recognize people only by their names, not through other characteristics. An extreme example was reported by the early explorers in *the Marquesas Islands. There it was possible for two people to exchange names as a sign of mutual respect. But this exchange of names also involved an exchange of responsibilities: obligations concerning the family, friends, and even enemies went with the change of name. A man might even be expected to go to war because of the (3) to his new name.

In some cultures, the use of a particular name is an offence. In imperial China, for instance, it was a crime to use the name of a reigning emperor. This could provide problems when the emperor's name was also a common word. If this occurred in an English-speaking country today where the emperor's name was (4), it would be illegal to talk about a (4) from the electricity company, a (4) before parliament, or the (4) of a bird. Similar prohibitions are found among *the Zulus: there a woman is not allowed to utter the name of her husband or the names of his parents.

Similar kinds of constraints can apply to the names of things, as well as to the names of people. It is fairly common to find a taboo against the use of the name of a powerful animal such as a bear, tiger, or crocodile. Instead, phrases like 'honey-eater' or nicknames like 'Bruin' are used. (5)<u>In parts of Africa and India it is not acceptable to call a snake a 'snake.'</u> Instead, you say things like 'There is a strap' or 'There is a rope.' It is believed that if you call something a snake, it is likely to act like a snake and bite you. In a similar way, *Bavarian farmers in Germany traditionally do not call a fox a 'fox,' in case using the word brings the fox and causes it to attack their hens. In a very similar way, we still say 'Talk of the devil,' suggesting that speaking of someone causes them to appear. Finally, and more subtly, it used to be the case in China that a doctor who did not have the appropriate drug for his patient would write the name of the drug on a piece of paper, burn it, and get the patient to eat the ashes. It was believed that the name of the drug would be just as effective as the drug itself.

（注） the Marquesas Islands：マルケサス諸島（フランス領ポリネシアの群島）
the Zulus：ズールー族（アフリカ南部に住むバンツー族に属する種族）
Bavarian：バイエルンの（バイエルンはドイツ南部の州）

(熊本県立大)

問1 空所(1)に入れるのに最も適当なものを，次のア～エから1つ選びなさい。

ア．adopted　イ．called　ウ．concealed　エ．disclosed

問2 下線部(2)を日本語に訳しなさい。

問3 空所(3)に入れるのに最も適当なものを，次のア～エから1つ選びなさい。

ア．reference　イ．responsibility　ウ．familiarity　エ．superiority

問4 空所(4)に共通して入る最も適当な1語を答えなさい。ただし，大文字で始めても，小文字で始めてもかまわない。

問5 下線部(5)の理由を50字以内の日本語で述べなさい。

問6 本文の内容と一致するものを，次のア～エから1つ選びなさい。

ア．ズールー族では，女性が自分の夫や自分の両親の名前を口にすることは許されていない。

イ．かつて中国では，医者が適切な薬を持っていないときに，その薬の名前を書いた紙を燃やしてその灰を患者に食べさせていた。

ウ．ドイツのバイエルンでは，「キツネ」という言葉が人間に病気をもたらすと信じられているので，動物のキツネを「キツネ」と呼ぶことを避けている。

エ．マルケサス諸島における最近の調査では，誰かと出会うとお互いの尊敬の証として必ず名前を交換することがわかった。

9

35 min.
558 words

次の英文を読んで，設問に答えなさい。

Fears about how robots equipped with artificial intelligence (AI) might transform our lives have been a classic part of science fiction for decades. (1)But these stories do not address AI's broader and potentially more significant *social* effects — the ways AI could affect how we humans interact with one another. Putting AI at the center of our lives may change how loving or friendly or kind we are — not just in our direct interactions with these machines, but in our interactions with one another.

Consider some experiments from my lab at Yale, where my colleagues and I have been exploring how such effects might play out. In (2)one study, we directed small groups of people to work with humanoid robots to lay railroad tracks in a virtual world. Each group consisted of three people and a small blue-and-white robot sitting around a square table, working on tablets. The robot was programmed to make occasional errors and to apologize for them: "Sorry, guys, I made a mistake this round," it declared cheerfully. "I know it may be hard to believe, but robots make mistakes, too." As it turned out, this clumsy confessional robot helped the groups perform *better* — by improving communication among the humans. They became more relaxed and conversational, comforting group members who made a mistake, and laughing together more often. Compared with the *control groups, whose robots made only basic statements, the groups with a confessional robot were better able to collaborate.

This study demonstrates that in systems where people and robots interact socially, the right kind of AI can improve the way humans relate to one another. But adding AI to our social environment can also make us behave less productively and less ethically.

In (3)another experiment designed to explore how AI might affect the "tragedy of the commons" — the notion that individuals' self-centered actions may collectively damage their common interests — we gave several thousand subjects money to use over multiple rounds of an online game. In each round, subjects were told that they could either keep their money or donate some or all of it to their neighbors. If they made a donation, we would also make a donation, doubling the money their neighbors received. Early in the game, two-thirds of players acted (4)altruistically. They realized that being generous to their neighbors in one round might prompt their neighbors to be generous to them in the next one, establishing a norm of *reciprocity. From a selfish and short-term point of view, however, the best outcome would be to keep your own money and receive money from your neighbors. In this experiment, we found that by adding just a few *bots (posing as human players) that behaved in a selfish way, we could drive the group to behave similarly. Eventually, the human players (5) cooperating altogether. The bots thus converted a group of generous people into selfish ones.

Let's pause to think about the implications of this finding. Cooperation is a key feature of our species, essential for social life. And trust and generosity are crucial in differentiating successful groups from unsuccessful ones. If everyone contributes and makes sacrifices in order to help the group, everyone should benefit. When this behavior breaks down, however, the notion of reciprocity disappears, and everyone suffers. The fact that AI might meaningfully reduce our ability to work together is extremely concerning.

（注） control group：対照群（実験で対照標準となるグループ）　reciprocity：互恵主義
bot：ボット（自動的に特定の仕事をするようにプログラムされたインターネット上のロボット）

（京都工芸繊維大）

問 1　下線部(1)を these stories の内容を明らかにして日本語に訳しなさい。

問 2　下線部(2)の実験結果から明らかになったことを80字以内の日本語で述べなさい。

問 3　下線部(3)の実験結果から危惧されることを30字以内の日本語で述べなさい。

問 4　下線部(4)とほぼ同じ意味を表すものを，次のア～エから１つ選びなさい。

ア．economically　　イ．greedily
ウ．unselfishly　　エ．egoistically

問5　空所(　5　)に入れるのに最も適当なものを，次のア～エから1つ選びなさい。

ア．liked　　イ．refused　　ウ．stopped　　エ．wanted

10

30 min.
477 words

次の英文を読んで，設問に答えなさい。

(1)<u>It is worth looking at one or two aspects of the way a mother behaves towards her baby</u>. The usual *fondling, *cuddling and cleaning require little comment, but the position in which she holds the baby against her body when resting is rather revealing. Careful American studies have disclosed that (2)<u>80 per cent of mothers cradle their infants in their left arms, holding them against the left side of their bodies</u>. If asked to explain the significance of this preference, most people reply that it is obviously due to the fact that more mothers are right-handed. By holding the babies in their left arms, the mothers keep their *dominant arm free for manipulations. But a detailed analysis shows that this is not the case. (3), there is a slight difference between right-handed and left-handed females, but not enough to provide an adequate explanation. It emerges that 83 per cent of right-handed mothers hold the baby on the left side, but then so do 78 per cent of left-handed mothers. In other words, only (4) per cent of the left-handed mothers have their dominant hands free for actions. Clearly there must be another less obvious explanation.

The only other clue comes from (5)<u>[the left side / the heart / the fact / that / is / of / on]</u> the mother's body. Could it be that the sound of her heart-beat is the vital factor? And in what way? Thinking along these lines it was argued that perhaps during its existence inside the body of the mother, the growing *embryo *becomes fixated on the sound of the heart-beat. If this is so, then the re-discovery of this familiar sound after birth might have a calming effect on the infant, especially as it has just been thrust into a strange and frighteningly new world outside. If this is so, then the mother, either instinctively or unconsciously, would soon arrive at the discovery that her baby is more at peace if held on the left against her heart, than on the right.

(6)<u>This may sound strange, but tests have now been carried out which reveal that it is nevertheless the true explanation</u>. Groups of new-born babies in a hospital nursery were exposed for a considerable time to the recorded sound of a heart-beat at a standard rate of 72 beats per minute. There were nine babies in each group and it was found that one or more of them was crying for 60 per cent of the time when the sound was not switched on, but that this figure fell to only 38 per cent when the heart-beat recording was *thumping away. The heart-beat groups also showed a greater weight-gain than the others, although the amount of food taken was the same in both cases. Clearly the beatless groups were burning up a lot more energy as a result of the vigorous actions of their (7).

（注） fondling：撫でてやること　cuddling：抱きしめてやること
dominant arm：利き腕　embryo：胎児
become fixated on A：Aを心の奥底に記憶する
thump away：ドキンドキンと鳴る

(Desmond Morris, *The Naked Ape: A Zoologist's Study Of The Human Animal*, Vintage Books)

(和歌山大)

問1　下線部(1)を日本語に訳しなさい。

問2　下線部(2)について，本文で正しい理由として挙げられているものを，次のア～エから１つ選びなさい。

ア．多くの母親が右ききだから。

イ．赤ん坊を左胸に抱く方が，母親にとって安全だから。

ウ．左胸に抱く方が赤ん坊は安らぐと，母親が感じとるから。

エ．左胸に赤ん坊を抱けば，母親は右手で用事をすることができるから。

問3　空所(　3　)に入れるのに最も適当なものを，次のア～エから１つ選びなさい。

ア．For example　イ．In addition　ウ．Therefore　エ．True

問4　空所(　4　)に入る最も適当な数字を答えなさい。

問5　下線部(5)の語(句)を文意が通るように並べ換えなさい。

問6　下線部(6)を日本語に訳しなさい。

問7　空所(　7　)に入れるのに最も適当なものを，次のア～エから１つ選びなさい。

ア．crying　イ．eating　ウ．sleeping　エ．listening

11

25 min.
447 words

次の英文を読んで，設問に答えなさい。

Humans have long conceived (1a) sentiments about sleep. We want it, enjoy it and despair when we can't get enough of it. Yet we also have a fear of getting too much. Napoleon recommended six hours of sleep each night for a man, seven for a woman and eight for a fool.

(2)Why do we need sleep, and how much of it should we get? Scientists are beginning to answer the questions, and believe that humans sleep for different reasons than other animals. In experiments, mice have been shown to suffer physically from lack of sleep. After a few days, they begin to lose weight, although they eat a lot. After 14 days, they die.

Humans, on the other hand, usually show few (1b) problems from lack of sleep. A bad night's sleep will cause little reduction in strength, *coordination or stamina. Yet (3)*cognitive function suffers sharply. Our vocabulary drops measurably; we are unable to concentrate for long periods; our speech may become unclear.

Why the difference between humans and other animals? Scientists reason that humans have learned to rest their bodies even in a waking state. The difference in *metabolic rate between a person lying down and one who is asleep may be as little as 5 percent. Yet our brains, it seems, very much need the rest that sleep provides.

The recommended amount of sleep has been disputed in recent years. Humans have strange sleep patterns, usually getting six to eight hours a night during the working week, and up to 10 on weekends. (4)[is / that / of us / why / more sleep / most / want / it] if we can get it?

(5a)American researchers now argue that humans need a minimum of nine hours' sleep each night. These scientists theorize that we are deprived of sleep most of the time. As proof, they cite the drowsiness most of us feel at some point during the day.

(5b)European researchers challenge this notion, asserting that there is such a thing as sleep *gluttony. The fact that we like sleep does not mean we need it.

Studies support the European view. If people are given the opportunity to sleep longer, for instance, they may not feel tired until a later hour the next day. The extra hour in bed may do nothing more than adjust our daily rhythm.

Experts say the drowsiness many of us feel during the day may not be because we had too little sleep at night, but because we need an early afternoon nap. (6)Humans were made to sleep not once, but twice, and a 10-minute nap after lunch will make most of us feel better. This is the reason so many cultures keep the siesta hour.

（注） coordination：（筋肉等の）調整能力　cognitive：認識の　metabolic rate：代謝率　gluttony：大食い

（福島大）

問1　空所(1a)(1b)に入れるのに最も適当なものを，次のア～エからそれぞれ１つずつ選びなさい。

(1a)　ア．positive　イ．negative　ウ．conflicting　エ．thoughtful

(1b)　ア．mental　イ．physical　ウ．scientific　エ．different

問2　下線部(2)に対する答えとして最も適当なものを，次のア～エから１つ選びなさい。

ア．肉体的機能が落ちるから。

イ．脳に休息が必要だから。

ウ．睡眠不足がひどくなると死ぬから。

エ．睡眠をとらないと体重が減るから。

問3　下線部(3)の具体的な内容を，日本語で３つ簡潔に述べなさい。

問4　下線部(4)の語（句）を文意が通るように並べ換えなさい。ただし，文頭にくるべき語も小文字で始められている。

問5　下線部(5a)(5b)の考え方として最も適当なものを，次のア～エからそれぞれ１つずつ選びなさい。

ア．We should take a 10-minute nap during the day.

イ．Most people need to sleep more hours a night than they actually do.

ウ．We should sleep as many hours as we like.

エ．Just because we like sleep, it doesn't mean we need to sleep.

問6　下線部(6)を日本語に訳しなさい。

12

35 min.
524 words

次の英文を読んで，設問に答えなさい。

"Don't look at the world with your hands in your pockets," Mark Twain once told an aspiring young author. "To write about it you have to reach out and touch it."

I thought of (1)<u>this advice</u> when I visited Robert Barnett, former executive director of the American Foundation for the Blind. Barnett was blinded at the age of 14 in an accident. As we chatted, he noticed, I don't know how, that I was gazing at a life-size bronze head of Helen Keller, which he keeps near his desk.

"Feel it with your hands," he told me. I ran my fingers over the cool metal. "Now does it look any different?" Barnett asked.

(2)<u>The difference was surprising</u>. The sculpture now had weight, depth, shape and character which had escaped my eyes.

"Touch is more than a substitute for vision," Barnett said. "It reveals qualities other senses can't even suggest. One of the greatest mistakes people make is thinking you have to be blind to enjoy it." Learning to develop the sense of touch is something like making your other senses secondary. (3)<u>In seeing with the eyes alone we are limited to what is immediately in front of us</u>. Touch along with vision enables us to see something as a whole.

Awareness of touch can bring a new feeling to the most (4) experiences. "I have just touched my dog," wrote the young Helen Keller in her diary. "He was rolling on the grass with pleasure in every muscle and limb. I wanted to catch a picture of him in my fingers, and I touched him lightly as I would cobwebs. But, to my surprise, his body turned towards me and moved into a sitting position, and his tongue gave my hand a lick. He pressed close to me as if he intended to put himself into my hand. He loved it with his tail, with his paw, with his tongue. If he could speak I believe he would say with me that paradise is attained by touch."

The sense of touch is capable of (5). Expert millers can recognize any grade of flour by rubbing a little between thumb and forefinger. A cloth expert can identify the coloring used in a cloth by the difference it makes in the texture. The blind botanist, John Grimshaw Wilkinson, learned to distinguish more than 5,000 species of plants by touching them lightly with his tongue.

(6)We are aware today of how important touch is to complete understanding of anything, and there are now museums that, instead of the old "Don't Touch" signs, offer children the chance to touch — to feel the roundness of a sculpture, the beautiful balance of an Inca pitcher, and the rough iron of an early New England kettle. Visitors to the Brooklyn Children's Museum are encouraged to pick up and handle the objects on display in every exhibit. "If they can't touch the things," says Michael Cohn, the museum's senior instructor of anthropology, "it is no different from watching a movie or TV show."

Maybe, as we all aim to enlarge the range of our impressions, our motto should be: (7)!

(岩手大)

問1 下線部(1)の内容を40字以内の日本語で述べなさい。

問2 下線部(2)の内容を50字以内の日本語で述べなさい。

問3 下線部(3)を日本語に訳しなさい。

問4 空所(4)に入れるのに最も適当なものを，次のア～エから1つ選びなさい。

ア．commonplace　イ．exciting　ウ．dangerous　エ．frightening

問5 空所(5)に入れるのに最も適当なものを，次のア～エから1つ選びなさい。

ア．basic distinction　イ．extraordinary development
ウ．emotional experience　エ．mystical prediction

問6 下線部(6)を日本語に訳しなさい。

問7 空所(7)に入れるのに最も適当なものを，次のア～エから1つ選びなさい。

ア．Feel free　イ．Look before you leap
ウ．Never give up　エ．Do touch

13

30 min.
515 words

次の英文を読んで，設問に答えなさい。

All of us, almost daily, experience the mobility of our world: we could be in Tibet tomorrow. And not only our bodies, but also our minds are traveling at the speed of light. Global communications have made us all (1a) neighbors and taught us tolerance. Two generations ago, there were no roads in Nepal; now the information superhighway and English language paths run through the teahouses of the Himalayas.

Yet even as we enjoy the opportunities of the borderless economy and the varieties of world music and our ability to appreciate the cultures of the world in our living rooms, we fail sometimes to consider where we are going or what we might be losing. "To be rooted," wrote the philosopher Simone Weil, "is perhaps the most important and least recognized need of the human soul." And in our dawning age of rootlessness, we tend to speed into the future (2)without counting the bends in the road.

One problem, of course, is that everything is happening so quickly. Five years ago is ancient history now, and yesterday scarcely prepares us for today. We have no (1b) examples to guide us. The classical poets Homer and Virgil sang of travelers, but not ones crossing 11 time zones before noon. And *nomads have always traveled across the earth, but on foot and in tune with the rhythm of the seasons and tradition. A new age of mobility means a new age of homesickness — and that is for those of us lucky enough to have a home.

All of us are (3) travelers now, able to fly in less than a day from the 21st century (downtown Tokyo, for example) to the 13th (Bhutan, where costumes, houses and customs are maintained in strict medieval style). Tonight we can fly into the depths of the (1c) season — or into the arms of a family we have not seen for 20 years. And the shrinking of distances in space may blind us to (4)the more significant distances that remain: flying from Beirut to Beijing to Bogota on successive days — and finding the same services in each — we may underestimate the differences in values and assumptions. The truths of the village square do not extend across the global village.

Thus traveling today can be like watching TV, channel surfing through a mass of images too fast to read and too various to sort. And traveling tomorrow, for those of us without a firm sense of neighborhood or community or home, may involve an even stronger sense of (1d) confusion. Our values like our bodies may be up in the air or lost in space. The only thing that can support the burden of our movement, after all, is a steadying sense of stillness. "Though we travel the world over to find the beautiful, we must carry it with us or we find it not," wrote the philosopher Emerson, who considered travel a "fool's paradise." The same is even truer of our sense of destination or home: (5)<u>whatever we find when we travel is only what we had inside us all along</u>.

（注） nomad：遊牧民

（立教大）

問１ 空所(1a)～(1d)に入れるのに最も適当なものを，次のア～エからそれぞれ１つずつ選びなさい。

ア．opposite　イ．virtual　ウ．previous　エ．spiritual

問２ 下線部(2)の意味として最も適当なものを，次のア～エから１つ選びなさい。

ア．所要時間など計算しないで

イ．頼りになる道連れもなく

ウ．先々のことは考えないで

エ．金銭的裏づけもないまま

問３ 空所(3)に入れるのに最も適当なものを，次のア～エから１つ選びなさい。

ア．time　イ．space　ウ．business　エ．fellow

問４ 下線部(4)の内容を30字以内の日本語で述べなさい。

問５ 下線部(5)を日本語に訳しなさい。

問６ 本文の内容と一致するものを，次のア～エから１つ選びなさい。

ア．We can't appreciate the cultures of the world by staying at home.

イ．In this age of borderlessness there are more rootless people.

ウ．When we watch TV, the fast changing images give us a good understanding of the world.

エ．Emerson thought that travel broadens people's minds.

14

30 min.
439 words

次の英文を読んで，設問に答えなさい。

We know that the two *cerebral hemispheres of the brain have different *cognitive capacities. (1)These can lead to asymmetries in behavior and in the way in which we interpret the world. Many studies suggest that the right hemisphere of the brain is more involved in the perception of emotion and in its expression than the left hemisphere of the brain.

In relation to language, the right hemisphere of the brain is better at interpreting the emotional tone of voice in speech. A typical experiment illustrates this. It uses some sentences with a happy message like "She won a prize" or "The sun is shining." Other sentences are (2a) cheerful; "He lost all his money gambling" or "It is raining very heavily," and yet other sentences are neutral with no particular emotional content. (3)They are read in different tones of voice, which are either consistent with the sentence's message or in opposition to it. Although in principle to lose money gambling is unpleasant, if it had happened to a great enemy it might nevertheless induce some sensation of pleasure, and it is possible to read the sentence "He lost all his money gambling" in a cheerful tone of voice. (2b), some Californians have an unusual enthusiasm for rain and it is possible to read the sentence "It is cold and rainy" in a cheerful tone of voice.

(4)Subjects are asked to categorize the emotional content of the sentence both in terms of the message that is conveyed and the tone of voice. Two sentences are presented at the same moment, one played to the right ear and one played to the left ear, in a listening set-up. Since the connections that the left ear makes with the right hemisphere are stronger than the connections the right ear makes with the right hemisphere, (5)any bias towards superior judgments from the left ear is taken as evidence of increased right-hemisphere involvement in the task. In this kind of experiment, the (6a) ear is better at making judgments about the tone of voice, whereas the (6b) ear is better at judging verbal content.

Brain-damaged patients who have sustained injuries to the (6c) hemisphere have difficulty in making such interpretations of emotional mood from speech. Their language and communicative systems appear relatively normal, in terms of being able to say roughly what they want to say, but the content of their speech is often emotionally flat, lacking its previous variation and *modulation and sounding rather (2c). In fact, it is suggested that the more creative elements in language are absent. Some of the *connotative associations of language may be influenced by the right hemisphere.

（注） cerebral hemisphere：大脳半球　cognitive：認識の　modulation：抑揚
connotative：言外の意味に関する

（専修大）

問 1　下線部(1)を日本語に訳しなさい。

問 2　空所(2a)～(2c)に入れるのに最も適当なものを，次のア～エからそれぞれ１つずつ選びなさい。

(2a)　ア．most　イ．more　ウ．as　エ．less

(2b)　ア．However　イ．On the contrary　ウ．Similarly　エ．Therefore

(2c)　ア．interesting　イ．dull　ウ．emotional　エ．normal

問 3　下線部(3)の内容として最も適当なものを，次のア～エから１つ選びなさい。

ア．よい内容の文は明るい調子で，悪い内容の文は暗い調子で読む。
イ．よい内容の文は暗い調子で，悪い内容の文は明るい調子で読む。
ウ．文の内容に関わらず，明るい調子と暗い調子のどちらかで読む。
エ．文の内容に関わらず，途中で声の調子を変えながら読む。

問 4　下線部(4)を日本語に訳しなさい。

問 5　下線部(5)を日本語に訳しなさい。

問 6　空所(6a)～(6c)のそれぞれに，left または right のいずれかを入れなさい。

15

30 min.
412 words

次の英文を読んで，設問に答えなさい。

One of the most remarkable stories I know is about a man called Robertson McQuilken. As a young man, he dreamed of becoming the president of Columbia Bible College in Columbia, South Carolina. He adored his father, who had held this position, and he hoped to take his father's place someday.

Robertson McQuilken's dream came true. One day he did become the president of Columbia Bible College. (1)When he became the president, he was convinced that he was called by God and was worthy of that position.

Dr. McQuilken served as president of that college for a number of years, and he did very well and was respected and loved by many people.

Then one day this man realized he had (2)a tragedy on his hands. His wife began to show the symptoms of Alzheimer's disease. She became worse in a short time, and in a matter of months she was in a terrible situation. She not only lost her memory of much of their life together, but she was unable to even recognize him. She lost all awareness that he was her husband.

Robertson McQuilken made his decision. He resigned the presidency of the college so he could give full-time care to his wife. Without hesitation, he walked away from his job as an act of love for her.

There were some realists who told him there was no meaning in (3)what he was doing. Anybody could take care of his poor wife, they told him, but not anybody could be president of the college. And after all, she didn't even recognize him when he came in the room to help her.

Then there were (4)some religious people who said he was walking away from what God called him to do. He was letting his personal concern for his wife (5) his more important social responsibility, they said.

The man's answers were magnificent. To the realists he admitted that his wife didn't know who he was. But that wasn't important, he told them. The really important thing was that he still knew who she was and, furthermore, (6)he let them know that he recognized in her now-forgetful self the same lovely woman he had married those many years ago.

Then he turned to the religious people. His words to them were even more profound: “There is only one thing more important than your job. And that is a promise. And I promised to be there ‘*until death do us part.’”

（注） until death do us part：死が二人を分かつまで（結婚式での誓いの言葉）

（大阪電通大）

問1 下線部(1)を日本語に訳しなさい。

問2 下線部(2)の内容を25字以内の日本語で述べなさい。

問3 下線部(3)の内容を20字以内の日本語で述べなさい。

問4 下線部(4)に対する Robertson McQuilken の答えを，20字以内の日本語で述べなさい。

問5 空所(　5　)に入れるのに最も適当なものを，次のア～エから1つ選びなさい。

ア．concentrate on　　イ．interfere with

ウ．make for　　エ．take up

問6 下線部(6)を them の内容を明らかにして日本語に訳しなさい。

問7 本文の内容と一致するものを，次のア～エから1つ選びなさい。

ア．Robertson was successful in realizing his dream of becoming the president of the college.

イ．Robertson had a dream that he would resign at an early age and his dream came true.

ウ．Robertson McQuilken quit his job because he became seriously ill.

エ．Realists said that Robertson McQuilken was irresponsible and selfish.

16

30 min.
479 words

次の英文を読んで，設問に答えなさい。

Here's everything you need to know about why Monday used to be so popular and what's made it so unpopular today. In fact, the day — originally named after the moon — was once (1) so much in England and the US that it was called "Saint Monday."

Back in the 18th and 19th centuries, the six-day workweek was standard in Britain and America. (2)<u>Workers only had Sundays off to go to church</u>, along with special holidays like Christmas and New Year that were scattered throughout the calendar. Even though Sunday was the only *official* weekly day of rest, many people still failed to show up on Monday. Many workers would stay home to recover from *hangovers after a drunken end to the workweek or just relax and devote some time to leisure. Thus, the phrase "keeping Saint Monday" was born. The habit caught on. According to the writer Witold Rybczynski, it became official practice for workers to take Monday off after a Friday or Saturday payday.

Saint Mondays acquired a somewhat bad reputation for being all about getting drunk, boxing, and *blood sports. However, (3)<u>the day didn't *just* involve hangovers or drinking away wages</u>. People would use their day off to visit horse races, cricket matches, public gardens, museums, theater productions, dance halls, and social club meetings.

Saint Monday allowed the working class valuable leisure time. In his paper "The Lower Classes and Politics 1800-1850," Michael Richards argues that the tradition gave workers the opportunity to "establish a degree of independence in relation to their employer." In his paper, "The Decline of Saint Monday," Douglas A. Reid refers to an 1851 London writer, who noted that the public gardens "were literally filled with well-dressed, happy and well-behaved working-class people. All appeared to greatly enjoy the glories of nature." So Saint Monday wasn't all about getting drunk.

Obviously, not everyone loved this custom. Business owners felt that the day off hurt their productivity. According to Reid's research, one factory owner moved his chemical works from Birmingham to Scotland in 1766, partly due to the custom of Saint Monday in England. As Rybczynski previously noted, in order to stop people from taking time off, shops and factories started closing earlier on Saturdays. (4)Reid adds that measures like allowing free Saturday afternoons, along with legislation, gradually weakened Saint Monday's dominance over the years.

Our current practice of a 40-hour workweek and two-day weekend has its roots in the Industrial Revolution and the gradual decline of Saint Monday. In 1908, a New England cotton mill established a two-day weekend on Saturday and Sunday, to allow both Jewish and Christian workers to worship on their respective holy days. However, (5)this model didn't fully catch on until *the Great Depression. This standard workweek is now widely accepted around the world. And thus, as the first day of the standard workweek, the once merry Monday was forgotten.

（注） hangovers：二日酔い　　blood sports：闘鶏などの流血を伴うスポーツ
the Great Depression：（1929年から始まった）世界大恐慌

（学習院大）

問1　空所(　1　)に入れるのに最も適当なものを，次のア～エから１つ選びなさい。

ア．ignored　　イ．hated　　ウ．loved　　エ．regarded

問2　下線部(2)の意味として最も適当なものを，次のア～エから１つ選びなさい。

ア．Only workers went to church on Sundays.

イ．Workers wanted to go to church on Sundays.

ウ．Workers had little time off for rest.

エ．Workers looked forward to special holidays.

問3　下線部(3)の具体的な理由を70字以内の日本語で述べなさい。

問4　下線部(4)を日本語に訳しなさい。

問5　下線部(5)が指す語句を同じ段落から抜き出しなさい。

問6　本文の内容と一致するものを，次のア～エから１つ選びなさい。

ア. Everyone approved of Saint Monday because the only days workers were allowed to rest were church holidays.

イ. Employers disliked the practice of Saint Monday because it encouraged workers to go to church.

ウ. The custom of Saint Monday in England was one reason for a factory owner moving his business to Scotland.

エ. Some people in England have continued the custom of Saint Monday since the Great Depression.

17

35 min.
561 words

次の英文を読んで，設問に答えなさい。

Starting about one million years ago, there was an increase in the growth of the human brain. It expanded at first at the rate of *one cubic inch every hundred thousand years; then the growth rate doubled; it doubled again; and finally it doubled once more. Five hundred thousand years ago the rate of growth hit its peak. At that time the brain was expanding at a rate of ten cubic inches every hundred thousand years. (1)No other organ in the history of life is known to have grown as fast.

What pressures generated the explosive growth of the human brain? (2) may supply part of the answer. At that time the world began to enter into a great Ice Age, the first on the planet in hundreds of millions of years. The trend toward colder weather set in slowly at first, but after a million years areas of ice began to form in the north. They thickened into glaciers as more snow fell, and then the glaciers joined together into great sheets of ice, as much as two miles thick. When the ice sheets reached their maximum extent, they covered two-thirds of the North American continent, all of Britain and a large part of Europe. Many mountain ranges were buried entirely. (3)So much water was locked up on the land in the form of ice that the level of the earth's oceans dropped by three hundred feet.

These events occurred precisely at the same time as the period of most rapid expansion of the human brain. Is this significant, or is it accidental?

The movements of humans in the last million years provide a clue to the answer. At the beginning of the Ice Age, humans lived near the equator, where the climate was mild and pleasant. Later they moved northward. From their birthplace in Africa they moved up across Arabia and then turned to the north and west into Europe, as well as eastward into Asia.

When (4)these early movements took place, the ice still only covered the lands in the far north; but eight hundred thousand years ago, the ice moved southward until it covered large parts of Europe and Asia. Then, for the first time, humans encountered the bone-chilling, freezing winds from the cakes of ice in the north.

The climate in southern Europe had a Siberian coldness then, and summers were nearly as cold as European winters are today.

In those difficult times, resourcefulness and inventiveness must have been of great value. Which individual first thought of stripping the fur from dead animals to wrap around his body? Only by (5)[human beings / imaginative acts / could / such inventive / survive / and] a cold climate. In every generation, the individuals with strength, courage, and creativity were the ones more likely to survive the Ice Age; those who were less resourceful fell victim to the climate and their numbers were reduced.

The Ice Age winter was the greatest challenge that humans had ever faced. They were naked and defenseless against the cold, as some little mammals had been defenseless against the dinosaurs one hundred million years before. Facing the pressures of a hostile world, both those mammals and humans were forced to live by their wits; and both became, in their time, the most intelligent animals of the day.

（注） one cubic inch：1立方インチ

（立教大）

問1 下線部(1)を日本語に訳しなさい。

問2 空所（ 2 ）に入れるのに最も適当なものを，次のア～エから1つ選びなさい。

ア. The custom of wearing clothes that took root in the first ice age

イ. The fact that human beings had to fight against dinosaurs

ウ. The invention of language and the use of tools

エ. A change of climate that set in about two million years ago

問3 下線部(3)を日本語に訳しなさい。

問4 下線部(4)の内容を50字以内の日本語で述べなさい。

問5 下線部(5)の語（句）を文意が通るように並べ換えなさい。

問6 本文の内容と一致しないものを，次のア～エから1つ選びなさい。

ア. The growth rate of the human brain hit its peak about 500,000 years ago.

イ. After the Ice Age began two million years ago, it took about one million years to form large areas of ice in the north.

ウ. Those with less resourcefulness and inventiveness couldn't survive the

Ice Age.

エ. Human beings during the Ice Age had nothing in common with small mammals one hundred million years ago.

18

30 min.
535 words

次の英文を読んで，設問に答えなさい。

Can the Polar Bear Survive?

The rapid shrinking of the Arctic ice cap is threatening the world's polar bear population, scientists have warned. Studies suggest the decline in the thickness and extent of the ice cap is causing the deaths of hundreds of bears a year. The total polar bear population is estimated at only 25,000. Many spend long periods trapped on land, where they find it hard to feed, rather than on ice, while young bears are dying in *dens that melt and collapse.

Research by Dr. Peter Wadhams shows that the summer ice now averages just 9 feet in thickness compared with 16 feet 20 years ago. He predicts that all the polar ice will disappear during the summer months by about 2080. However, the bears will suffer disastrous declines long before then. Around Hudson Bay in Canada the increasing warmth has forced bears onto land when the ice melts from July to October. In recent years, however, the return of the ice has been delayed by up to a month — leaving dozens of underweight and hungry bears roaming on the beaches waiting for its return. The animals cannot easily find food on land, so every day spent (1)<u>waiting</u> means that they consume more fat reserves.

Scott Schliebe said huge changes in the biology of the Arctic were apparent. "The *pack ice is already diminishing every summer and without pack ice I cannot see how the bears would survive. They are not adapted for living on land," he said. (2)<u>The bears live almost entirely on floating ice that packs together to create vast expanses separated by small areas of open water that they swim across</u>. They are superbly adapted for survival in the frozen north, eating mainly *seals. They range across a huge area of ice controlled by Russia, America, Canada, Greenland, and Norway. Adult males reach weights of 1,500 pounds and are among the fiercest and most dangerous of animals.

Bears have long been hunted by humans for meat and fur. The numbers to be destroyed are now strictly controlled by international agreements but hundreds are still killed each year. Humans also present another threat to bears —

through pollution of the sea with poisonous chemicals called PCBs, which accumulate in fat. (3)The huge layers of fat used by bears to survive in the cold collect PCBs, which then affect their *hormonal systems and can cause sex changes.

Scientists say the warming of the Arctic is largely due to rising global temperatures. The direct effect is to melt the ice from above — but the indirect effect is even more destructive. Wadhams' research shows that *the Gulf Stream and other currents that carry warm water north have become stronger, warming water beneath the ice cap to melt it from below, too. Another effect of the melting ice will be to open up the shipping routes between Europe, northern Russia and the Far East and to end the annual winter isolation of Siberia. "In the next few years we are going to see the opening up of the Arctic Ocean to year-round traffic," said Wadhams. "Eventually the northwest passage around Canada may open up, too. It will completely alter our trading patterns — but for bears the future could be (4)."

（注） den：巣穴　pack ice：浮氷群（流氷が寄り集まってできた氷原）
seal：アザラシ　hormonal system：内分泌系
the Gulf Stream：メキシコ湾流

（滋賀県立大）

問1　下線部(1)の waiting について，何が何を待っているのか，日本語で簡潔に述べなさい。

問2　下線部(2)を日本語に訳しなさい。

問3　下線部(3)を日本語に訳しなさい。

問4　空所(4)に入れるのに最も適当なものを，次のア～エから1つ選びなさい。

ア．bright　イ．rosy　ウ．dark　エ．promising

問5　ホッキョクグマの数が減少している原因として本文中で述べられていないものを，次のア～エから1つ選びなさい。

ア．気候の温暖化。
イ．人間による狩猟。
ウ．水質汚染。
エ．他の動物による殺りく。

問6　Wadhams および Schilebe の見解に含まれないものを，次のア～エから1つ選びなさい。

ア．数年のうちに，北極海が１年を通じて通行可能となる。

イ．北極の氷の厚さが20年前に比べてほぼ半分になっている。

ウ．浮氷群がなくなったとしても，ホッキョクグマは生きていける。

エ．ホッキョクグマの数は，近い将来に壊滅的に減少するだろう。

19

30 min.
439 words

次の英文を読んで，設問に答えなさい。

I feel like I'm losing my mind. Over the last few years, I've had an uncomfortable feeling that someone, or something, has been changing the way my brain works. I haven't completely lost my mind, but I can feel it's changing. I feel it most strongly when I'm reading. (1)I used to find it easy to get lost in a book or a long article, but that's rarely the case anymore. Now my concentration starts to drift after a page or two. I read a little bit, then start looking for something else to do. I feel like I'm always pulling my lazy brain back to the text.

I think I know what's going on. For well over two decades now, I've been spending a lot of time online, searching and surfing the internet. I'm a writer, so the internet (2) me a lot of time when I'm doing research. I use my computer to pay bills, schedule appointments, book flights and hotel rooms, and do many other tasks. Even when I'm not working, I'm reading and writing emails, scanning headlines, flicking through Instagram, watching short videos on YouTube, or just jumping from link to link.

These are all advantages, both for work and play. Such easy access to information! But these advantages come at (3)a price. The internet is not only a channel of information. It also shapes our thought processes. And what the internet seems to be doing is reducing my ability to concentrate and think. Whether I'm online or not, my mind now expects to take in information the way the internet sends it to me: in a fast-moving stream of tiny information packets. My calm, focused mind is being pushed aside by a new kind of mind that wants to take in information in short, unrelated, and overlapping bursts — the faster the better.

Recently, a research company published a study of the effects of internet use on young people. The company interviewed 6,000 college students who have grown up using the internet and reported that (4)the internet has affected the way the young people absorb information. "They don't necessarily read a page from left to right and from top to bottom. They might instead skip around, scanning for important information of interest.”

We humans used to have a ‘linear’ mind — a mind that was good at processing long, difficult text, without losing concentration. But now, that’s changing. For the last five centuries, ever since the printing press made book reading a popular activity, the linear mind has been the center of art, science, and society. Now, that mind may be (5).

(北星学園大)

問1 下線部(1)を日本語に訳しなさい。

問2 空所(2)に入れるのに，s で始まる最も適当な1語を答えなさい。

問3 下線部(3)はどういうことか，日本語で述べなさい。

問4 下線部(4)はどういうことか，80字以内の日本語で具体的に述べなさい。

問5 空所(5)に入れるのに最も適当なものを，次のア～エから1つ選びなさい。

ア．useful only for writers

イ．more important than ever

ウ．a thing of the past

エ．a cause of a reading disorder

20

30 min.
480 words

次の英文を読んで，設問に答えなさい。

(1)<u>Language serves many functions</u>. Certainly one of its most common and most important purposes is to help us describe various phenomena, such as events, situations, and people: "What is it?" Another purpose is to evaluate these same phenomena: "Is it good or bad?" Typically, we consider descriptions to be objective, whereas we consider evaluations to be subjective.

But is the distinction between objective description and subjective evaluation a clear one? The answer, in the vast majority of cases, is no. Why? Because words both describe and evaluate. (2)<u>When we attempt to describe something or someone, the words we use almost always carry values, in that they reflect our own personal likes and dislikes</u>. Thus, our use of any particular term serves not only to describe, but also to assert what is desirable or undesirable to us.

This problem is not so prevalent in the physical sciences, as compared to the social sciences. Let's take, as an illustration, the terms cold and hot. In the field of physical sciences, both terms refer, in a relatively neutral sense, to the rate of *molecular vibrations (or temperature): "That liquid is very cold," or "That liquid is very hot." When we use these same terms to describe an individual, however, they take on a distinctly evaluative meaning: "That person is very cold," or "That person is very hot."

What are the consequences of the evaluative bias of language? The words that we use can, with or without intention, become powerful instruments of change. In those instances where we are deliberately attempting to influence others to agree with our point of view, we intentionally select words that most persuasively communicate our values. In many cases, however, the process is unintentional. Our best attempts to remain neutral are restricted by (3)<u>the limits of language</u>. When it comes to describing people it is nearly impossible to find words that are empty of evaluative meaning. (4)<u>[may / as / it / incredible / seem]</u>, we simply don't have neutral adjectives to describe personality characteristics. And even if such words did exist, we still would be very likely to utilize the ones that reflect our own personal preferences.

This also emphasizes the (　5　) influence of attitudes and language. That is, not only do our attitudes and perceptions affect our use of language, but our use of language in turn influences our attitudes and perceptions.

Because of the evaluative bias of language, we must be careful both to become aware of our own personal values and to communicate these values as openly and fairly as possible. In other words, we should avoid presenting our value judgments as objective reflections of truth. We should also be alert to the value judgments inherent in other people's use of language, and in many cases the words they use tell us at least as much about (6)<u>them</u> as about the events and individuals they are attempting to describe.

（注）　molecular：分子の

（一橋大）

問 1　下線部(1)の many functions について，本文中に述べられているものを２つ日本語で簡潔に述べなさい。

問 2　下線部(2)を日本語に訳しなさい。

問 3　下線部(3)の内容として最も適当なものを，次のア～エから１つ選びなさい。

ア．適切な言葉を見つけることが不可能なこと。

イ．言葉には必ず評価的意味が伴うこと。

ウ．自分の価値観を伝える言葉を意図的に選ぶこと。

エ．言葉の選択が意図的ではないこと。

問 4　下線部(4)の語を文意が通るように並べ換えなさい。ただし，文頭にくるべき語も小文字で始められている。

問 5　空所(　5　)に入れるのに最も適当なものを，次のア～エから１つ選びなさい。

ア．indirect　　イ．limited　　ウ．cultural　　エ．mutual

問 6　下線部(6)が指しているものを英語で答えなさい。

24X20

河合塾
SERIES

改訂版

やっておきたい英語長文500

［解答・解説編］

河合塾講師
杉山 俊一
塚越 友幸
山下 博子
［共著］

河合出版

はじめに

大学の入試問題では、読解問題が最も大きな割合を占めていますし，その割合はますます高くなっています。読解問題を解けるようにすることは，受験を突破するうえで避けては通ることができません。それでは，読解問題を解くためには，どのような力が必要なのでしょうか。語い力に加えて，一文一文の構造を正確に捉え，内容を把握する力が必要です。さらに，複数の文が集まって文章が構成されている以上，文と文のつながり，すなわち文脈を読み取る力も必要です。また，今日的な話題が出題されることが増えています。そうした話題について知っておくことも，内容を理解するためには大切です。

こうした力をつけるためには，何よりも良い英文を読み，良い問題を解くことです。そこで，これまでに出題された問題の中から，英文の長さと難易度を基準に繰り返し読むに値する英文を選び，4冊の問題集にまとめました。設問は，ある文章に対して問うべきこと—内容の理解と英語の理解—という観点から，ほぼ全面的に作り変えてあります。

やっておきたい英語長文500は，最も出題頻度の高い**400語から600語**の標準からやや難しいレベルの英文20題で構成されています。内容の理解を問う客観問題から和訳問題，内容説明問題まで幅広く扱うことで，**ほとんどの大学の読解問題に対応できる高度な読解力の養成**を目指します。また，設問を解く際の着眼点や考え方，論旨の展開を読み取るうえで知っておくべきことを Advice としてまとめてあります。

やっておきたい英語長文500を終えた人は，**やっておきたい英語長文700**に挑戦してください。

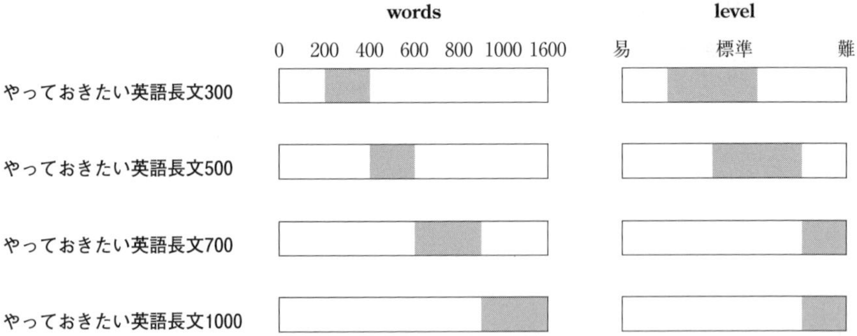

本書が皆さんの想いの実現に向けて，役に立つことを願ってやみません。それでは，問題1にトライしてみましょう。

最後に，本書を改訂するにあたり，Kathryn A. Craft 先生に英文校閲を行っていただきました。この場を借りて御礼申し上げます。

著者記す

本書の使い方

1　問題には語数と標準解答時間を示してあります。標準解答時間を目標に問題を解いてください。

2　解説には，解答と設問解説，要約，構文・語句解説があります。設問解説を読み，解答を確認してください。設問解説中の第１・２段落第５文といった表記は，構文・語句解説の番号に対応しています。

3　構文・語句解説では，訳例と設問解説で触れなかった，構文および語句の解説があります。設問以外の箇所で理解できなかった部分を確認してください。

4　構文・語句解説では，問題文から下線を省き空所を埋めた形で英文を再録してあります。英文を繰り返し読んでもらいたいからです。こうすることが，速読の練習にもなりますし，語いの定着にもつながります。また，このときは，英文の構造よりも，内容・論旨を追うことを心がけてください。確認のために要約を活用してください。

5　英文を読む際には，音読とリスニングを組み合わせることで，リスニング力も強化できます。英語のネイティブ・スピーカーが読み上げた音声が用意されていますので，利用してください。

音声は，パソコンやスマートフォンから下記の URL にアクセスして聴くことができます。QR コードからもアクセスできます。

https://www.kawai-publishing.jp/onsei/01/index.html

・ファイルは MP4形式の音声です。再生するには，最新版の OS をご利用ください。

また，パソコンから URL にアクセスしていただくことで，音声データのダウンロードも可能です。

※ホームページより直接スマートフォンへのダウンロードはできません。パソコンにダウンロードしていただいた上で，スマートフォンへお取り込みいただきますよう，お願いいたします。
・ファイルは ZIP 形式で圧縮されていますので，解凍ソフトが必要です。
・ファイルは MP3形式の音声です。再生するには，Windows Media Player や iTunes などの再生ソフトが必要です。
・Y501～Y520の全20ファイル構成となっています。

<音声データに関する注意>
・当サイトに掲載されている音声ファイルのデータは著作権法で保護されています。本データあるいはそれを加工したものを複製・譲渡・配信・販売することはできません。また，データを使用できるのは，本教材の購入者がリスニングの学習を目的とする場合に限られます。
・お客様のパソコンやネット環境により音声を再生できない場合，当社は責任を負いかねます。ご理解とご了承をいただきますよう，お願いいたします。
・ダウンロードや配信サイトから聴くことができるのは，本書を改訂するまでの期間です。

本書で用いた記号

- （　）は省略可能な語句を表す。
- [ ]は直前の語句と書き換え可能な語句を表す。
- S は主語，O は目的語，C は補語を表す。
- A, B は名詞を表す。
- X, Y は文の中で同じ働きをするものを表す。
- *do* は動詞の原形を表す。
- to *do* は不定詞を表す。
- *doing* は動名詞または現在分詞を表す。
- *done* は過去分詞を表す。
- *one's* は主語と同じ所有格を表す。
- A's は主語と同じになるとは限らない所有格を表す。
- 「自動詞＋前置詞」型の熟語は，account for A のように表す。
- 「他動詞＋副詞」型の熟語は，put A off のように表す。
- 他動詞は，solve「を解く」のように表す。

目　次

Advice

1 日本語による内容一致問題

2 英語による内容一致問題

3 タイトル選択問題

4 下線部和訳問題

5 内容説明問題①　指示語 this

6 内容説明問題②　指示語 that

7 内容説明問題③　the same / similar / opposite

8 内容説明問題④　原因・理由の説明

9 語い問題

10 ディスコース・マーカー①

11 ディスコース・マーカー②

12 具体例，体験談，引用

13 比喩表現

14 実験・調査の紹介

15 物語文

16 論説文　主題－展開型①

17 論説文　主題－展開型②

18 論説文　主題－展開型③

19 論説文　導入－主題－展開型

20 論説文　主題－展開－結論型

適度なストレス

解　答

問1　エ

問2　そのことについて考えれば考えるほど，ストレスには私たちにとって何か価値があるように思われた。

問3　イ. make up for

問4　do I start working seriously to get the job done

問5　エ. a desire for improvement

問6　ストレスの多い活動を長期間要求する方針を持っている会社に雇われている人たちは，同情に値する。なぜならあまりに多くのストレスは逆効果を招くからである。

問7　イ

▶▶▶ 設問解説 ◀◀◀

問1　this advice の具体的内容は第1段落第2・3文に述べられている。

問2　全体の構造は，the＋比較級 ...，the＋比較級～「…すればするほど，ますます～」の表現を用いたもの。it seemed that ... は「…だと思われた」という表現。また，there is の後ろに省略された語句を補うと there is some value for us in it となる。in it の it は stress を指す。

問3　第3段落第4文の「1年中きちんと勉強すれば，心配などせずに試験に臨める」という内容と，空所の前の「しかし実際には，ほとんどの学生はできるだけ最後まで勉強をしない」という内容から「無駄にした時間を埋め合わせる」となるようにイを選ぶ。

ア.「を廃止する」イ.「を埋め合わせる」ウ.「を我慢する」エ.「を切らす」

問4　only のついた副詞節が文頭にきているため倒置(疑問文の語順)の形が起きる。よって，do I start が確定する。次に，第4段落第2文の「クリスマスカードや手紙を遅くまで放っておいて，楽に終えられなくなると気づく」という内容から「緊張が高まってはじめて，仕事を終わらせるために真剣に働き始める」という意味の英文が求められていることがわかる。

例　Only when he left me did I realize how much I loved him.
「彼が去ってはじめて，私はどれほど彼を愛していたかわかった」

□ start *doing*「…し始める」　□ seriously「真剣に」

□ get O *done*「Oを…してしまう」

問5 下線部の具体的な内容は直後のダッシュ以下に述べられている。また，下線部を含む文の構造は What has been called “divine discontent”(S) produces(V) progress(O) である。したがって，divine discontent とは，「何であれ現在の状況への創造的な不満であり，進歩を生み出すもの」ということになる。

ア.「精神的な病気」　イ.「ストレスへの無関心」

ウ.「道義についての不満」　エ.「改善に対する願望」

□ divine「神聖な」　□ discontent「不満」

問6 who are ... stressful activity は主語 Those of us を修飾する関係代名詞節。また，whose policies ... stressful activity は関係詞節中にある a company を修飾する関係代名詞節である。なお，those は those who ...「…する人たち」の形でよく用いられ，ここでは「私たちのうちの…する人たち」が逐語訳。動詞 are to be sympathized は be＋to 不定詞の表現で，ここでは可能を表し「同情できる」という意味になる。since 以下は主節の理由を述べている。

□ employ「を雇う」　□ policy「方針／政策」　□ demand「を要求する」

□ since S V ...「…ので」　□ counterproductive「逆効果の」

問7 ア. 本文に記述なし。

イ. 本文全体，特に第５・８段落の内容に一致。

ウ. 第１段落第２・３文の内容に不一致。

エ. 第５段落第２文の内容に不一致。

Advice 日本語による内容一致問題

内容一致問題の選択肢が日本語で与えられている場合は，まず選択肢に目を通してみること。繰り返し使われている語句に着目することで，今から読むことになる英文の内容に関するヒントが得られるはずである。本問では，選択肢の「ストレス」という語に着目すれば「ストレスの影響」について論じられた文章であると予測することができる。日本語の選択肢がない場合でも，英文を読む前に設問に目を通すようにしたい。設問の指示文から，英文の内容を推測できることがあるし，設問によっては最初から答えを探して本文を読むこともできる。

要　約

園芸の専門家が植物にストレスを与えると美しい花を咲かせると言っていたが，人間の場合もストレスが進歩を生むこともある。事前に準備があれば，ある程度のストレスはよい結果を生むために必要であるかもしれない。(100字)

構文・語句解説

第１・２段落

[1]Listening to a gardening program the other day, I was struck by something the expert said about a particular type of potted plant. [2]Do not water it once it has come into bud, he advised. [3]Cause it to feel stress, and it will produce more, and more beautiful, flowers.

[4]Surely this advice is against everything that we are told by doctors. [5]Stress is bad for us, they say. [6]Stress is the cause of all sorts of diseases. [7]Stress caused by overwork sometimes results in early death. [8]Newspaper and magazine articles tell us how to reduce stress, or how to avoid it altogether. [9]No one has a good word for stress.

[1]先日，園芸の番組を聞いていて，ある種の鉢植え植物について専門家が言ったことに感心した。[2]いったん芽を出したら，その植物には水をやるなとその人は忠告したのだ。[3]ストレスを感じさせると，より多く，しかもより美しい花を咲かせるのだと。

[4]確かにこの忠告は，私たちが医者に言われることのすべてに反するものである。[5]医者が言うには，ストレスは身体によくない。[6]ストレスはあらゆる種類の病気の原因なのである。[7]働き過ぎによるストレスは，ときには早死にという結果になる。[8]新聞や雑誌の記事はストレスを減らす方法とかストレスを完全に避ける方法を教えてくれる。[9]ストレスに対してよいことを言う人はいない。

1 Listening to ... day は時を表す分詞構文。
the expert ... potted plant は something を修飾する関係代名詞節。
□ gardening「園芸」　□ the other day「先日」　□ be struck「感心する」
□ expert「専門家」　□ potted plant「鉢植えの植物」

2 Do not ... into bud および Cause it ... flowers は専門家が忠告した内容。
□ water「に水をやる」　□ once S V ...「いったん…すると」

3 Cause it ..., and it will ... は，命令文, and ...「…しなさい，そうすれば〜」の表現。
□ cause O to *do*「Oに…させる」　□ produce「を生む」

4 □ surely「〈文修飾で〉確かに」　□ against A「Aに逆らって，反して」

6 □ sort「種類」　□ disease「病気」

7 □ result in A「Aという結果になる」

8 □ article「記事」　□ reduce「を減らす」　□ altogether「完全に」

9 □ have a good word for A「Aをほめる」

第3段落

[1]And yet, I asked myself, if stress is good for plants, can there possibly be any value for us in it? [2]The longer I thought about it, the more it seemed to me that there is. [3]Without a certain degree of tension and stress, we are apt to become lazy and neglect our duties. [4]All students know that they should study regularly throughout the year, and then be able to face examinations without fear. [5]In fact, most students leave this study till the last possible moment, and then hastily try to make up for lost time.

[1]しかし，私は自問した。ストレスが植物によいなら，その中にはひょっとすると私たちにとっても何か価値があるのではないか。[2]そのことについて考えれば考えるほど，ストレスには私たちにとって何か価値があるように思われた。[3]ある程度の緊張やストレスがなければ，私たちは怠け者になってやるべきことをおろそかにしがちである。[4]学生はみんな１年じゅうきちんと勉強すれば，心配などせずに試験に臨めることを知っている。[5]しかし実際には，ほとんどの学生はできるだけ最後まで勉強をしないでおいて，無駄にした時間をあわてて埋め合わせようとする。

1 if stress ... ? の疑問文は筆者が自問した内容である。in it の it は stress を指す。

□ and yet「しかし」　□ ask *oneself*「自問する」　□ possibly「ひょっとしたら」

3 □ certain A「あるA」　□ degree「程度」　□ tension「緊張」

□ be apt to *do*「…しがちである」　□ neglect「を怠る」

□ duty「〈複数形で〉務め，職責」

4 know の目的語の that 節は文末までで，study regularly ... と be able ... が and で結ばれている。

□ throughout A「Aの間じゅう，Aを通じて」　□ face「に直面する」

5 □ leave「を放っておく」　□ hastily「あわてて」

第4段落

[1]Many of us, likewise, put off dealing with our problems until the deadline approaches. [2]Every year I resolve that I will write all my Christmas cards and letters ahead of time, and avoid a last-minute rush; and every year I find that once again I have left it too late for me to finish comfortably. [3]Only when the tension increases do I start working seriously to get the job done.

[1]同様に，私たちの多くも期限が近づくまで問題に対処するのを引き延ばす。[2]毎年，私はクリスマスカードや手紙をすべて早めに書いて，最後になってあわてないようにしようと決心する。そして毎年またしても気づいてみると，遅くなるまで放っておいて，楽に終えられなくなってしまう。[3]緊張が高まってはじめて，仕事を終わらせるために真剣に働き始めるのだ。

1 □ likewise「同様に」　□ put A off「Aを延期する」
□ deal with A「Aを扱う，処理する」　□ deadline「期限，締め切り」
2 too late for me to finish は too ... to *do*「とても…なので～できない」の表現を用いたもので，for me は to finish の意味上の主語。
□ resolve that 節「…ということを決意する」　□ ahead of time「〈予定より〉早く」
□ last-minute「土壇場の」　□ rush「あわただしさ」　□ comfortably「心地よく」

第5・6段落

[1]In other fields too, when satisfaction enters in, creativity and curiosity go out of the window. [2]What has been called "divine discontent"—a creative dissatisfaction with the present situation, whatever it is—produces progress. [3]And that dissatisfaction is one type of stress.

[4]Thus, it seemed to me, a certain degree of stress is necessary for human progress. [5]Just how much is good, and how much is harmful, is the problem.

[1]他の分野でも満足が入ってくると創造性や好奇心は窓から出ていってしまう。[2]「神聖な不満」と呼ばれているもの—何であれ現在の状況への創造的な不満—は，進歩を生み出す。[3]そのような不満も一種のストレスなのである。

[4]したがって，ある程度のストレスは人間の進歩にとって必要であると思える。[5]いったいどれくらいがよくて，どれくらいが有害なのかが問題なのだ。

1 □ field「分野」　□ enter in「入り込む」　□ creativity「創造性」　□ curiosity「好奇心」
2 whatever it is は「譲歩」を表す副詞節。it は the present situation を指す。
□ dissatisfaction「不満」　□ the present A「現在のA」　□ situation「状況」
□ progress「進歩」　4 □ thus「したがって」
5 Just は疑問詞を強調して「いったい」という意味。how much ... で始まる2つの疑問詞節が and で結ばれている。　□ harmful「有害な」

第７・８段落

[1]Those of us who are employed by a company whose policies demand long periods of stressful activity are to be sympathized with, since too much stress is counterproductive. [2]Those of us who are self-employed may have more freedom to choose our own best level of stress. [3]In either case, we need some preparation before the period of stress in order to be able to succeed.

[4]So, like the potted plant in question, if we are watered sufficiently to begin with, and then left to struggle for a while on our own, we too may produce more and better flowers than one who, over-protected, has never had to try.

[1]ストレスの多い活動を長期間要求する方針を持っている会社に雇われている人たちは，同情に値する。なぜならあまりに多くのストレスは逆効果を招くからである。[2]自営業の人たちは自分に最適なレベルのストレスを選ぶ自由はより多いかもしれない。[3]どちらの場合も，うまくできるようになるにはストレスが生じる前にいくらか準備をしておく必要がある。

[4]というわけで問題の鉢植えのように，私たちもはじめに十分に水が与えられ，それからしばらくの間，自力でがんばるように放っておかれると，過保護にされて努力をする必要がなかった人より，より多く，しかもよりよい花を咲かせるかもしれないのである。

2 □ self-employed「自営の」　□ freedom to *do*「…する自由」

3 either case「どちらの場合も」とは，第７段落第１・２文で述べられた「会社に雇われている場合」と「自営の場合」のこと。

□ preparation「準備」

4 are watered ... begin with と left to ... our own が and で結ばれている。

who, over-protected, has never had to try は one を修飾する関係代名詞節で，over-protected は分詞構文。

one＝a person

□ A in question「当のＡ，例のＡ」　□ sufficiently「十分に」

□ to begin with「初めに」　□ leave O to *do*「Ｏに…させておく」

□ struggle「がんばる，奮闘する」　□ for a while「しばらくの間」

□ on *one's* own「一人で／独力で」　□ over-protected「過保護にされた」

カモノハシ

解答

問1　誰かオーストラリアのおもしろくもない悪ふざけをする人が，オーストラリア大陸の距離と新奇さを利用して，はなはだしく異なる動物の様々な部分を縫い合わせて，英国の何も知らない動物学者をばかにしようと躍起になっているのだ。

問2　哺乳動物のように体に毛が生えていながら，水鳥のようなくちばしと足，ヘビのような毒のかぎづめ，卵を産むような穴が後部にあったから。(64字)

問3　内臓器官を調べることが可能な状態で標本を受け取ったとき，心臓はまさに哺乳動物のものに似ており，爬虫類のものとはまったく似ていないように思われた。

問4　platypus は学名としてすでに使われていたため重複は許されなかったから。

問5　エ，カ，ク

設問解説

問1　全体の文構造は，Some unfunny joker in Australia(S) ... , had stitched(V_1) ... and was(V_2) intent(C) ... である。なお，Some の訳出に注意。some は単数形の名詞の前で用いられて，「〈具体的にはわからない〉誰か，ある」という意味を表す。主語の後ろの taking advantage ... the continent は主語に補足説明を加える現在分詞句で，S, *doing* ... , V は「Sは…し，Vする」と訳出すればよい。

例　His mother, smiling softly, asked if she could be of any help.
「彼の母は優しく微笑んで，何かお手伝いしましょうかと聞いた」

□ unfunny「おもしろくない」　□ joker「悪ふざけをする人，いたずら者」
□ take advantage of A「Aを利用する」　□ strangeness「未知，新奇さ」
□ continent「大陸」　□ stitch A together「Aを縫い合わせる」
□ widely「はなはだしく，ひどく」　□ creature「動物」
□ be intent on *doing*「…することに没頭している，熱中している」
□ make a fool of A「Aをばかにする」　□ innocent「何も知らない」
□ zoologist「動物学者」

問2　下線部(2)は「爬虫類の特徴を持つ哺乳動物なのか，それとも哺乳動物の特徴を持つ爬虫類なのか，あるいは一部が鳥なのか，いったい何なのか」という意味である。it は第1・2段落第1文で述べられた英国に送られてきた1つの剥製のことであり，英国の動物学者がその剥製を見て下線部(2)のような疑問を抱いた理由は，第1・2段落第7～10文で述べられている。したがって，この内容を制限字数内でまとめる。

□ mammal「哺乳動物」　□ reptilian「爬虫類の」　□ characteristic「特徴」

□ reptile「爬虫類」　□ mammalian「哺乳動物の」　□ partly「一部分は」

問3 in such condition as to make it possible to study the internal organs は「内臓器官を調べることが可能な状態で」という意味。it は形式目的語で，to study the internal organs が真目的語である。主節は it appeared that ...「…と思われた」の表現で，that 節内の and は just like ... と not at all ... を結んでいる。また，2つの those はともに the hearts のこと。

□ specimen「標本」　□ receive「を受け取る」　□ internal organ「内臓器官」

□ heart「心臓」　□ be like A「Aに似ている」　□ not at all「まったく…でない」

問4 第5・6段落第3文に *Platypus anatinus* と名づけられた理由が述べられ，第5・6段落第5文には，「それが *Ornithorhynchus paradoxus* に変更された」と述べられている。therefore「それゆえに」に着目すれば，変更の理由がその前の第4文に述べられていることがわかる。よって，その内容を簡潔にまとめればよい。

問5 ア.「オーストラリアから持ち込まれた動植物はすべてなじみのあるもので，カモノハシも例外ではなかった」第1・2段落第2文および第9・10段落第5文の内容に不一致。

イ.「19世紀末までに動物学者はカモノハシの生態をすでに完全に理解していた」第9・10段落第5文の内容に不一致。

ウ.「卵を作る仕組みのように思われたものは，泳ぐための器官であるとわかった」第7・8段落第3文に関連するが，「泳ぐための器官」とは述べられていないので不一致。

エ.「哺乳動物ではあるが，カモノハシ以外にも卵を産む動物がいることが発見された」第9・10段落第2文の内容に一致。

オ.「カモノハシは限られた水温域にしか棲息できないことが今ではわかっている」第9・10段落第6文の内容に不一致。

カ.「初めてカモノハシが持ち込まれたとき，腹を立てる人もいたし，作り物だと考えた人もいたし，信じられない面持ちでじっと見つめる人もいた」第1・2段落第6文および第3・4段落第1・2文の内容に一致。

キ.「動物学者はその剥製の動物がどこで生まれたのかについて何十年も激しく

議論を続けた」第5・6段落第1文に関連するが，第6文に述べられているように議論したのは本物かどうかについてなので不一致。

ク.「あるメッセージによって，モントリオールにいる英国の科学者に，カモノハシ以外の毛の生えた動物が産んだ卵がある，と伝えられた」第9・10段落第2文および第4文の内容に一致。

Advice 英語による内容一致問題

英語による内容一致問題の選択肢には，かなり紛らわしいものや，英文全体の内容の読み取りに関するものもあるが，選択肢の作り方にはいくつかの典型的なパターンがある。1．**否定表現**（部分否定や not や never を用いない否定表現に注意），2．**頻度や限定の副詞**（特に always や only に注意），3．**数量表現**（特に all や every に注意），4．**比較表現**（何と何をどのような基準で比較しているかに注意），5．**仮定法**（直説法の内容を仮定法で問う）などがポイントになっていることが多い。したがって，上記の表現には特に注意して選択肢と本文の対応箇所をよく読んで，落ち着いて解答することが大切である。本問の問5のアでは否定表現に，オでは only に注意すること。

要　約

オーストラリア大陸から奇妙な動物の剥製が英国に届き，その正体をめぐって様々な議論がなされたが，20世紀になってようやくその生態が明らかとなった。それはカモノハシと呼ばれる卵生の哺乳動物であった。(96字)

構文・語句解説

第1・2段落

[1]In 1800, a stuffed animal arrived in England from the newly discovered continent of Australia. [2]The continent had already been the source of plants and animals never seen before — but this one was ridiculous. [3]It was nearly two feet long, and had fur-covered skin. [4]It also had a flat rubber-like bill, a piece of skin between its toes, a broad flat tail, and a spur on each hind leg that was clearly intended to produce poison. [5]What's more, under the tail was a single opening.

[6]Zoologists stared at the thing in disbelief. [7]Hair like a mammal! [8]Bill and feet like an aquatic or water bird! [9]Poison spurs like a snake! [10]A single opening in the rear as though it laid eggs!

[1]1800年に，新たに発見されたオーストラリア大陸から英国に１つの剥製の動物が届いた。[2]すでにオーストラリア大陸は今まで一度も見たことのない植物や動物の宝庫となっていた。しかし，これはとんでもない代物だった。[3]体長は２フィート近くあり，毛に覆われた皮を持っていた。[4]また平たいゴムのようなくちばし，足の指の間には皮膚のようなもの，幅広い平らなしっぽがあり，そして明らかに毒を出すためのかぎづめが後ろ足のどちらにもあった。[5]おまけにしっぽの下にはたった１つの穴があった。

[6]動物学者は信じられない面持ちでその物を見つめた。[7]哺乳動物のような毛！[8]水生動物，つまり水鳥のようなくちばしと足！[9]ヘビのような毒のかぎづめ！[10]卵を産むかのような後部の１つの穴！

2 this one の one は stuffed animal のこと。

☐ source「源泉，源」　☐ ridiculous「ばかげた，とんでもない」

3 ☐ fur-covered「毛皮に覆われた」　☐ skin「皮膚／皮」

4 ☐ flat「平たい」　☐ rubber-like「ゴムのような」　☐ bill「くちばし」　☐ toe「足の指」

☐ hind「後ろの」　☐ be intended to *do*「…するためのものである」

☐ produce「を出す，生む」　☐ poison「毒」

5 under the tail was a single opening は副詞句＋V＋S の語順。

☐ what's more「そのうえ」

6 ☐ stare at A「Aをじっと見る」　☐ in disbelief「信じられずに」

8 or water の or は言い換えを表し「つまり」という意味。

例　I saw a puma, or American lion in the zoo.「私は動物園でピューマつまりアメリカライオンを見た」

☐ aquatic「水生の」

10 ☐ rear「後ろ」　☐ lay an egg「卵を産む」

第３・４段落

[1]There was an explosion of anger. [2]The thing was a joke. [3]Some unfunny joker in Australia, taking advantage of the distance and strangeness of the continent, had stitched together parts of widely different creatures and was intent on making fools of innocent zoologists in England.

[4]Yet the skin seemed to fit together. [5]There were no signs of artificial joining. [6]Was it or was it not a fake? [7]And if it wasn't a fake, was it a mammal with reptilian characteristics, or a reptile with mammalian characteristics, or was it partly bird, or what?

[1]怒りが爆発した。[2]それは悪ふざけだ。[3]誰かオーストラリアのおもしろくもない悪ふざけをする人が，オーストラリア大陸の距離と新奇さを利用して，はなはだしく異なる動物の様々な部分を縫い合わせて，英国の何も知らない動物学者をばかにしようと躍起になっているのだ。

[4]しかし，皮はぴったりと合っているようだった。[5]人工的に縫い合わせた痕跡はなかった。[6]模造品なのだろうか，それとも模造品ではないのだろうか。[7]また，もしそれが模造品でないのなら，爬虫類の特徴を持つ哺乳動物なのか，それとも哺乳動物の特徴を持つ爬虫類なのか，あるいは一部が鳥なのか，いったい何なのか。

1 □ explosion「爆発」

4 □ seem to *do*「…するように思われる」　□ fit together「ぴったりと合う」

5 □ sign「痕跡，形跡」　□ artificial「人工的な」　□ joining「つなぎ合わせること」

6 □ fake「模造品」

第5・6段落

[1]The discussion went on heatedly for decades. [2]Even the name emphasized the ways in which it didn't seem like a mammal despite its hair. [3]One early name was *Platypus anatinus*, which is Latin for "Flat-foot, duck-like." [4]Unfortunately, the term "platypus" had already been applied to a type of beetle and there could be no duplication in scientific names. [5]It therefore received another name, *Ornithorhynchus paradoxus*, which means "Bird-beak, paradoxical."

[6]Slowly, however, zoologists had to reach agreement and admit that the creature was real and not a fake, however upsetting it might be to zoological notions. [7]For one thing, there were increasingly reliable reports from people in Australia who caught glimpses of the creature alive. [8]The *paradoxus* was dropped and the scientific name is now *Ornithorhynchus anatinus*.

[1]議論は何十年も激しく続いた。[2]毛があるにもかかわらず哺乳動物らしからぬその姿を，その名前までもが強調していた。[3]初期の名前はプラティプス・アナティヌスであった。これは「平たい足の，アヒルのような」を表すラテン語である。[4]残念なことに，「プラティプス」という言葉はすでにある種のカブトムシに適用されており，科学用語には重複は許されていなかった。[5]そのため，それはオルニソリンクス・パラドクサスというほかの名前をもらうことになった。これは「鳥のくちばしの，逆説的な」という意味である。

[6]しかし，どんなにそれが動物学的観念を揺るがすようなものであろうと，動物学者たちは次

第に合意に達し，その動物が本物であり模造品ではないことを認めざるをえなかった。[7]1つには，生きたその動物を見かけたオーストラリアの人々から，ますます信頼できる報告が寄せられてきたからである。[8]パラドクサスは取り下げられ，今では科学名は「オルニソリンクス・アナティヌス」である。

1 □ go on「続く」　□ heatedly「激しく」　□ decade「10年」

2 □ emphasize「を強調する」　□ seem like A「Aのように思われる」

3 □ Latin「ラテン語の」

4 □ term「用語」　□ apply A to B「AをBに適用する」　□ beetle「カブトムシ」
□ duplication「重複」

6 however upsetting ... zoological notions は，was real, not a fake を修飾する譲歩を表す副詞節。
□ agreement「合意」　□ upsetting「動揺させるような」

7 □ for one thing「1つには」　□ increasingly「ますます」　□ reliable「信頼できる」
□ catch a glimpse of A「Aをちらっと見る」

8 □ drop「を捨てる，除く」

第7・8段落

[1]To the general public, however, it is the “duckbill platypus,” or even just the duckbill, the queerest mammal (assuming it is a mammal) in the world.

[2]When specimens were received in such condition as to make it possible to study the internal organs, it appeared that the heart was just like those of mammals and not at all like those of reptiles. [3]The egg-forming machinery in the female, however, was not at all like that of mammals, but like that of birds or reptiles. [4]It seemed really and truly to be an egg-layer.

[1]しかし，一般の人にとっては，それは「ダックビル・プラティプス」またはただのダックビルであり，世界一奇妙な哺乳動物(哺乳動物と仮定してのことだが)である。

[2]内臓器官を調べることが可能な状態で標本を受け取ったとき，心臓はまさに哺乳動物のものに似ており，爬虫類のものとはまったく似ていないように思われた。[3]しかし，雌が卵を作る仕組みは哺乳動物のものとはまったく違っており，鳥類か爬虫類のものに似ていた。[4]それは本当に産卵する動物のように思われた。

1 □ the general public「一般大衆」　□ queer「奇妙な」

□ assume (that)節「…だと仮定する」

3 □ machinery「仕組み」　□ female「雌」

□ not X but Y「XではなくY」X，Yには like で始まる前置詞句がきている。

4 □ really and truly「本当に，まさに」　□ egg-layer「産卵する動物」

第9・10段落

[1]It wasn't till 1884, however, that the actual eggs laid by a creature with hair were found. [2]They were not the eggs of a platypus, but another Australian species, the spiny anteater. [3]That was worth an excited announcement. [4]A group of British scientists were meeting in Montreal at the time, and the egg-discoverer, W. H. Caldwell, sent them a message to announce the finding.

[5]It wasn't till the twentieth century that the intimate life of the duckbill came to be known. [6]It is an aquatic animal, living in Australian fresh water at a wide variety of temperatures — from tropical streams at sea level to cold lakes at an elevation of a mile.

[1]しかし，1884年にはじめて毛のある動物から実際に産まれた卵が発見された。[2]その卵はカモノハシの卵ではなく，もう１つのオーストラリア種であるハリモグラの卵であった。[3]それは興奮のうちに発表されるに値した。[4]ある英国の科学者グループがそのときモントリオールで会合を開いていたのだが，卵の発見者 W. H. コールドウェルは彼らにその発見を知らせるメッセージを送ったのだ。

[5]20世紀になってはじめてカモノハシの詳しい生態が知られるようになった。[6]それは，海面レベルの熱帯の川から１マイルもの高度にある冷たい湖にいたるまでの，実に様々な温度の所で，オーストラリアの淡水に生息する水生動物である。

1 □ it isn't till ... that ～「…してはじめて～する」

2 They were not the eggs of a platypus, but another Australian species は not X but Y「XではなくY」を用いたもので，They were the eggs of not a platypus, but another Australian species の not が前に出た形となっている。another Australian species と the spiny anteater は同格の関係。

□ species「種」

3 □ be worth A「Aに値する」　□ announcement「発表」

5 □ intimate「詳しい」　□ come to *do*「…するようになる」

6 living in ... of temperatures は分詞構文。ダッシュ以下は at a wide variety of temperatures の

内容を具体的に述べたもの。

□ fresh water「淡水」　□ a variety of A「様々なA」　□ tropical「熱帯の」

□ stream「川」　□ sea level「海水面」　□ elevation「高度，海抜」

3 子どもの手書き文字

解　答

問1　我々の手書き文字は，自分が手紙を書いている相手が好きかどうかによって変わるかもしれない。

問2　ウ．Of course not

問3　「不器用」と言われる子どもは，そのような子どもが受けるべき治療を受けた後でさえ，体操や球技で秀でることは決してないかもしれないと認めることに学校は慣れているのかもしれない。

問4　for conditions over which they have little

問5　子どもが乱雑な字を書くことを繰り返し批判されると，生まれつきの不器用さに緊張が加わること。(45字)

問6　ウ．legible and fast

問7　イ．Handwriting tells a lot about a writer

▶▶▶ 設問解説 ◀◀◀

問1 It は直前の文の主語 Our own handwriting を指す。depending on A「A次第で」の A に whether 節がきている。we are writing to は the person を修飾する関係代名詞節。

□ alter「変わる」　□ write to A「Aに手紙を書く」

問2 直前の文では supposing (that) 節「もし…ならば」を用いて述べられた3つの場合に「自分の書く文字が変わらないままだと期待できるだろうか」と疑問を投げかけている。第1段落第1～3文に述べられているように，「私たちの筆跡は精神状態や疲れなどに左右される」ので，疑問文に対する答えは「もちろんそんなことは期待できない」となる。したがって，正解はウ。

ア.「それは依存する」 イ.「それが起こることだ」

ウ.「もちろんそんなことは期待できない」 エ.「きっとそうだ」

問3 be accustomed to *doing* は「…することに慣れている」の意味。that 以下は accepting の目的語となる名詞節。termed ‘clumsy’ は children を修飾する過去分詞句。that such children deserve to receive は the therapy を修飾する関係代名詞節。

□ accept「を受け入れる，認める」　□ term O C「OをCと呼ぶ」

□clumsy「不器用な」　□excel at A「Aに秀でている」　□gymnastics「体操」
□game「球技」　□therapy「治療」　□deserve to *do*「…するのに値する」
□receive「を受け取る」

問4 第2段落第2・3文では，「運動神経が悪いと，筆跡にも表れる」ことが述べられている。下線部(4)を含む文の前半には「ぎこちない手はぎこちない文字を書かせる可能性が高い」と述べられているので，後半は「子どもは自分ではほとんどどうしようもない症状のことで叱られるべきではない」という意味になるように for conditions over which they have little とする。over which 以下は conditions を修飾する関係代名詞節。have control over A の over が関係代名詞 which とともに節の先頭にきている。
□scold A for B「BのことでAを叱る」　□have control over A「Aを制御する」

問5 下線部(5)を含む文は「これは事態を悪化させるだけである」という意味。したがって，何が事態を悪化させるのか，つまり「何がさらに子どもがうまく書けないようにする」のかを考えればよい。下線部の直前の文に「もし子どもが『乱雑な』字を書くことを繰り返し批判されるなら，生まれつきの不器用さに緊張が加わる」とあるので，「緊張すればさらに子どもはうまく書けなくなる」と考えられる。したがって，This は直前の文全体の内容を指す。

問6 空所(6)を含む部分は，形容詞・副詞＋enough for A to *do*「Aが…するほど〜」の表現である。「書いている子どもが授業で遅れずについていくことができるほど手書き文字がどのようなものであれば，子どもが褒められるのに値する」のかを考えればよい。したがって，正解はウ。なお，legible は難単語であるが，他の選択肢が不適切であることから答えは得られる。
ア.「簡素だがゆっくりとした」イ.「小型だが合理的な」ウ.「判読可能で速い」
エ.「複雑で凝った」

問7 本文全体にわたって「手書き文字が様々なことを判断する手段となる」ことが述べられている。したがって，正解はイ。
ア.「上手な文字は成功につながる」
イ.「手書き文字は書き手について多くを語る」
ウ.「文字をよりうまく書く方法」
エ.「子どもが書いたもの」

Advice タイトル選択問題

タイトル選択問題では，英文全体の主題を押さえることが大切である。各段落に述べられている個々のトピックを捉えつつ，すべての段落に共通する主題を押さえなければならない。本問の問7のエのように，英文全体を通して述べられているものの，主題としては適切でないものをタイトルとして選ばないこと。この英文では「手書き文字が様々なことを判断する手段となる」ことが，子どもが書いたものを例に挙げて述べられている。ここから英文全体を貫く主題がどのようなものであるのかを判断すること。

要 約

筆跡は発達段階や精神状態などの診断ツールとなるが，子どもは字が汚いと非難されると緊張が加わり，さらに汚い字を書くことになる。判読可能であれば褒めると，子どもの自己イメージアップにもつながる。(95字)

構文・語句解説

第１段落

[1]Handwriting is a valuable diagnostic tool. [2]It gives a measurable and permanent indication of the writer's stage of development, and sometimes their state of mind, at any particular moment. [3]Our own handwriting, for instance, may change when we are tired or tense. [4]It may alter depending on whether we like the person we are writing to or not. [5]However, there would be more fundamental differences to our usual writing if real problems were involved. [6]Supposing we had an accident and had to learn to write with our non-preferred hand; supposing we developed an illness that left us with a tremor; or supposing we suffered a nervous breakdown, would we expect our handwriting to remain unchanged? [7]Of course not, so we should realize that the writing of children who may be suffering from any of a wide variety of conditions will reflect these conditions. [8]In the classroom they are often expected to be able to attain the same level of handwriting as pupils with no similar problems. [9]If we could look at handwriting problems as an indicator and a diagnostic tool instead of measuring problem handwriting against some mythical norm, this would be a positive and major step forward.

[1]手書き文字は貴重な診断ツールである。[2]それは，その時々のそれを書いた人の発達段階や，時に精神状態を示す計測可能で永続的な指標となる。[3]たとえば，自分自身の手書き文字は，疲れているときや緊張しているときには変わるかもしれない。[4]自分が手紙を書いている相手が好きかどうかによって変わるかもしれない。[5]しかし，もし本当に問題がある場合，通常の筆跡にもっと根本的な違いが現れるであろう。[6]事故に遭い，利き手でない方の手で書けるようにならなければならない場合，病気を発症して手が震えるようになった場合，あるいは神経衰弱を患っている場合，自分の手書き文字が変わらないままだと期待できるだろうか。[7]もちろん

そんなことは期待できない。だから，様々な症状のいずれかに苦しんでいるかもしれない子どもの手書き文字がその症状を反映することを認識すべきである。[8]教室では，彼らは自分と似通った問題を持っていない生徒と同レベルの手書き能力を獲得できると期待されることが多い。[9]もし根拠のない基準に照らして，問題のある手書き文字を評価する代わりに，手書き文字の問題を1つの指標や診断ツールとして見ることができるなら，これは前向きで大きな前進の一歩となるだろう。

1 □ handwriting「手書き文字，筆跡」　□ valuable「貴重な，役に立つ」
□ diagnostic「診断の」　□ tool「道具，手段」

2 2つめの and は the writer's stage of development と their state of mind を結んでいる。
□ measurable「測定可能な」　□ permanent「永続的な」　□ indication「指標，しるし」
□ stage「段階」　□ development「発達」　□ state「状態」　□ mind「精神，心」
□ particular「特定の」　□ moment「時期，場合」

3 □ *one's* own A「～自身のA」　□ for instance「たとえば」　□ tense「緊張した」

5 仮定法過去の文。
□ however「しかし」　□ fundamental「根本的な」　□ difference「違い」
□ usual「通常の」　□ *one's* writing「筆跡」　□ real「本当の」
□ involve「を関係させる」

6 3つの supposing がセミコロンおよび or で並列されており，仮定法過去の条件節となっている。that left us with a tremor は an illness を修飾する関係代名詞節。
□ learn to *do*「…できるようになる」　□ non-preferred「好ましくない」
□ develop「〈病気など〉になる」　□ illness「病気」　□ leave A with B「AにBを残す」
□ tremor「震え」　□ suffer「を経験する，こうむる」　□ nervous breakdown「神経衰弱」
□ expect O to *do*「Oが…するのを期待する」　□ remain C「Cのままである」

7 who may ... of conditions は children を修飾する関係代名詞節。
□ realize that 節「…だと認識する」　□ suffer from A「Aに苦しむ，悩む」
□ a wide variety of A「多様なA」　□ condition「症状」　□ reflect「を反映する」

8 with no similar problems は pupils を修飾する前置詞句。
□ attain「を成し遂げる」　□ the same A as B「Bと同じA」　□ pupil「生徒」
□ similar「類似した」

9 仮定法過去の文。and は an indicator と a diagnostic tool を結んでいる。
□ as A「Aとして」　□ indicator「指標」　□ instead of *doing*「…する代わりに」
□ measure「を測定する，評価する」　□ against A「Aと照らし合わせて」
□ mythical「神話の，根拠のない」　□ norm「基準」　□ positive「前向きな」
□ major「主な」

第2段落

[1]Schools may be accustomed to accepting that children termed ‘clumsy’ may never excel at gymnastics or games, even after the therapy that such children deserve to receive. [2]If these children’s motor co-ordination is such that they find difficulty, for example, in catching a ball, then this awkwardness will quite likely be reflected in their handwriting. [3]They may never be able to produce the neat, conventional handwriting that some teachers expect. [4]Awkward hands are likely to produce awkward handwriting, so children should not be scolded for conditions over which they have little control. [5]If they are repeatedly criticized for producing ‘untidy’ written work, then tension will be added to their natural clumsiness. [6]This will only make the situation worse. [7]Of course, any practical advice that might assist the writer, especially in the way of changes in writing posture, should be given. [8]Apart from that, providing the handwriting is legible and fast enough for the writer to keep up in class, surely those children deserve praise for the way they are tackling a job that is more difficult for them than for others. [9]A positive attitude is most likely to relax the writer. [10]This relaxation will probably be reflected in their written work, and any resulting praise will help to improve the self-image of these children who daily have to see their best efforts condemned as untidy.

[1]「不器用」と言われる子どもは，そのような子どもが受けるべき治療を受けた後でさえ，体操や球技で秀でることは決してないかもしれないと認めることに学校は慣れているのかもしれない。[2]もしこのような子どもの運動神経が非常に悪くて，たとえば，ボールを捕るのが困難であるなら，この不器用さはおそらく手書き文字に反映されるだろう。[3]彼らは一部の教師が期待するような，きちんとした型通りの字を書くことがまったくできないかもしれない。[4]ぎこちない手はぎこちない文字を書かせる可能性が高い。だから子どもは自分ではほとんどどうしようもない症状のことで叱られるべきではない。[5]もし子どもが「乱雑な」字を書くことを繰り返し批判されるなら，生まれつきの不器用さに緊張が加わる。[6]これは事態を悪化させるだけである。[7]もちろん，文字を書く子どもを助けるような，特に書くときの姿勢を変えるような実際に役立つどんな忠告をも与えるべきである。[8]そのうえ，書いている子どもが授業で遅れずについていくことができるほど手書き文字が判読可能で速く書かれていれば，そのような子どもは他の子どもにはそうではなくても彼らにとっては難しいことに取り組んでいるという点で，間違いなく褒めるのに値する。[9]前向きな姿勢は書き手の心を落ち着かせる可能性が非常に高い。[10]このような落ち着きはおそらく彼らが書くものに反映されるだろう。そしてその結果，褒めてもらえれば，最善を尽くしているのに乱雑だと毎日非難されなければならない子どもの自己

イメージを高めるのに役立つであろう。

2 If ..., then ～ は「もし…するならそれなら～」という表現。

□ motor co-ordination「運動神経」　□ be such that S V ...「大変なものなので…」

□ for example「たとえば」　□ awkwardness「不器用さ」

□ quite likely「たぶん，おそらく」

3 that some teachers expect は the neat, conventional handwriting を修飾する関係代名詞節。

□ produce「を産み出す」　□ neat「きちんとした」　□ conventional「従来型の」

□ expect「を期待する」

4 □ awkward「ぎこちない」　□ be likely to *do*「…する可能性が高い」

5 第2文と同じ If ..., then ～ の表現。

□ repeatedly「繰り返して」　□ criticize A for B「AをBのことで批判する」

□ untidy「乱雑な」　□ tension「緊張」　□ add A to B「AをBに加える」

□ natural「生まれつきの」　□ clumsiness「不器用さ」

6 □ situation「状況」

7 that might assist the writer は any practical advice を修飾する関係代名詞節。might は婉曲の用法で「たぶん…だろう」という意味。

□ practical「実際的な」　□ especially「特に」　□ change in A「Aの変更」

□ posture「姿勢」

8 that is more difficult for them than for others は a job を修飾する関係代名詞節。

□ apart from A「Aに加えて」　□ providing「もし…ならば」

□ keep up「遅れずについていく」　□ surely「確かに」　□ deserve「に値する」

□ praise「賞賛」　□ the way S V ...「…するやり方，方法」　□ tackle「に取り組む」

9 □ attitude「姿勢，態度」　□ relax「をくつろがせる」

10 who daily have to see their best efforts condemned as untidy は these children を修飾する関係代名詞節。see their best efforts condemned は see O *done*「Oが…されるのを目にする」の表現。

□ relaxation「(心身の) くつろぎ，息抜き」　□ resulting「結果として生じる」

□ help to *do*「…するのに役立つ」　□ improve「を向上させる」

□ self-image「自己イメージ」　□ daily「毎日」

□ condemn O as C「OをCとして非難する」

4 Eメールの影響

解答

問1　エ. the way we want to

問2　Eメールが直接連絡をとる方法として受け入れられているから。(29字)

問3　視覚信号や聴覚信号がないと，話し手が自分に関して他人に知られてもかまわない情報の量が大幅に増加するのである。

問4　ア. seeing yourself

問5　我々が知っているようなEメールは高度なプライバシーを与えてくれ，次にそうしたプライバシーが隠し立てしなくなるのに役立つのである。

問6　イ. accurate and complete

設問解説

問1　コロン(：)以下の内容「人に声を聞かれたり，顔を見られたりしないで，意思を伝達することができる」から，意味を推測する。

ア.「他人の利益になるように」イ.「他人にやって欲しいやり方で」ウ.「自分の言葉で」エ.「自分が望むやり方で」

問2　下線部(2)は「電話番号ではなく，Eメールのアドレスを公表する傾向が高まりつつある」という意味。直後の文に This practice is a result of とあり，This practice とは，下線部(2)の「Eメールのアドレスを公表する」慣習のことである。したがって，the increasing acceptance 以下の内容を制限字数内でまとめればよい。

□ tendency to *do*「…する傾向」

問3　The lack of visual and auditory signals(S) increases(V) the amount of information(O)という構造。speakers are 以下は information を修飾する関係代名詞節。「視覚信号や聴覚信号の欠如が，話し手が自分に関して他人に知られてもかまわない情報の量を大幅に増加させる」が直訳。auditory は難語ではあるが，下線部(3)が前の文の内容を一般化して述べたものであることが読み取れれば，If there is no voice to hear and no face to see から「聴覚の」という意味であることが推測できる。

□ lack「欠如」　□ visual「視覚の」　□ auditory「聴覚の」　□ signal「信号」

□ be willing to *do*「…するのをいとわない」　□ let O *do*「Oに…させてやる」

問4 空所(4)を含む文に述べられた研究については，第4段落第3・4文でその方法が説明され，第5文に結果が述べられている。第5文に「鏡のある部屋にいると，個人的な情報を話さなかった」とあるので，「自分の姿が見えるとプライバシーの感覚が減少する」ことが実証されたのである。

ア.「自分の姿が見えること」イ.「自分の声が聞こえること」ウ.「他人の姿が見えること」エ.「他人の声が聞こえること」

問5 接続詞の as で導かれた節には直前の名詞を限定する働きがある。ここでは，as we know it が直前の E-mail を限定して，「我々が知っているようなEメール」という意味。which 以下は，直前の a high degree of privacy を修飾する非制限用法の関係代名詞節。また，ここでの in turn は「順番に」ではなく「今度は，次に」という意味。

例 Modern life as we know it is unnatural to human beings.

「我々が知っているような現代の生活は人間にとって不自然なものである」

□ allow「を与える」 □ degree「程度」 □ help (to) *do*「…するのに役立つ」

□ generate「を生じる」 □ openness「隠し立てしないこと」

問6 空所(6)を含む文の文頭には Similarly「同様に」とあるので，第3～5段落で述べられた「プライバシーが守られることによって，自分に関する情報を隠し立てしなくなる」ということが「コンピュータの役割」に関しても言えると考えられる。

ア.「不正確で偏った」イ.「正確で完全な」ウ.「公式で最近の」エ.「一般的で興味深い」

Advice 下線部和訳問題

下線部和訳問題では，まず文の構造を正確に捉えることが大切である。主語，動詞，目的語，補語といった文を構成する要素と修飾語句を正確に把握すること。次に文脈を踏まえて何を言っているのか，つまり内容を考える。基本的には文構造に忠実な訳でかまわないが，日本語として不自然な場合は自然な日本語になるように工夫する必要がある。もちろん，個々の語の訳出に関しては文内容から最もふさわしい訳語を考えなければならない。また，本問の問3のように，難語があっても，文脈を踏まえて文内容を読み取ることができれば，その意味を推測することができる。

要　約

Eメールはプライバシーを保護し，顔見知りでない人と連絡をとるのにも使われるようになっている。また，プライバシーが守られることによって，自分に関する情報を隠し立てしなく

なる傾向がある。(91字)

構文・語句解説

第1段落

[1]It's interesting how much e-mail affects our personal space. [2]While some businesses have replaced much inter-office phone communication with e-mail, most users see e-mail as a medium that protects their private space far more than the telephone. [3]E-mail gives us the freedom to communicate on our own terms: it's possible for us to communicate without allowing anyone to hear our voice or see our face.

[1]Eメールが個人空間にいかに影響を及ぼすかということは興味深い。[2]社内電話の多くをとり止めEメールを使うようになった企業もあるが，Eメールを使っている人はたいていEメールは電話よりもずっと私的空間を保護してくれる伝達手段であるとみなしている。[3]Eメールは自分の都合に合わせて意思を伝達する自由を与えてくれる。人に声を聞かれたり，顔を見られたりしないで，意思を伝達することができるのである。

1 It's interesting how much ... の It は形式主語で，真主語は how much 以下。

☐ e-mail「Eメール／にEメールを送る」 ☐ affect「に影響を及ぼす」

☐ personal space「個人空間」

2 ☐ while S V ...「…する一方で」 ☐ replace A with B「AをBと取り替える」

☐ inter-office phone communication「社内電話」 ☐ see O as C「OをCとみなす」

☐ medium「伝達手段，媒体」 ☐ private space「私的空間」

3 ☐ the freedom to *do*「…する自由」 ☐ allow O to *do*「Oが…するのを可能にする」

第2段落

[1]While e-mail offers personal privacy, it also enables us to start a conversation with people we aren't acquainted with. [2]We send e-mail to people we would rarely telephone or request to see face-to-face. [3]Of course, the people we send messages to have the option to respond at their own convenience — or not at all. [4]There is a growing tendency to make e-mail addresses, but not phone numbers, public. [5]This practice is a result of the increasing acceptance of e-mail as a form of direct contact, even with well-known people we usually couldn't approach in person.

[1]Eメールは個人のプライバシーを与えてくれる一方で，Eメールによって顔見知りでない人と話を始めることもできる。[2]めったに電話をしなかったり，直接会ってくれるように頼むことのないような人にEメールを送る。[3]もちろん，メッセージを送った相手は，自分の都合で返信する選択の自由があるし，まったく返信しなくてもかまわないのである。[4]電話番号ではなく，Eメールのアドレスを公表する傾向が高まりつつある。[5]このような慣習は，Eメールが，普段じかに接することがないような有名人とでも，直接連絡をとる方法としてますます受け入れられるようになっている結果なのである。

1 we aren't acquainted with は people を修飾する関係代名詞節。

□ enable O to *do*「Oが…することを可能にする」

□ be acquainted with A「Aと知り合いである」

2 we would rarely telephone or request to see face-to-face は people を修飾する関係代名詞節。

□ rarely「めったに…しない」　□ request to *do*「…するように願い出る」

□ face-to-face「面と向かって(の)」

3 we send messages to は the people を修飾する関係代名詞節。

not at all＝have the option not to respond at all

□ the option to *do*「…する選択の自由」　□ at *one's* own convenience「自分の都合で」

□ not at all「まったく…でない」

5 we usually couldn't approach in person は well-known people を修飾する関係代名詞節。

□ practice「慣習」　□ the acceptance of A as B「AをBとして受け入れること」

□ form「形式」　□ approach「に接する」　□ in person「本人が直接に」

第3段落

[1]If there is no voice to hear and no face to see, many e-mail users become very open about the information they are willing to reveal on-line. [2]The lack of visual and auditory signals greatly increases the amount of information speakers are willing to let others know about themselves. [3]People write things in e-mails they would not want to say in a face-to-face conversation or on the telephone.

[1]耳に入る声や目に見える顔がなければ，Eメールを使う人の多くは，オンラインで明らかにしてもかまわない情報に関して隠し立てしなくなる。[2]視覚信号や聴覚信号がないと，話し手が自分に関して他人に知られてもかまわない情報の量が大幅に増加するのである。[3]人は面と向かっての会話や電話では言いたくないようなことを，Eメールには書く。

1 they are willing to reveal on-line は the information を修飾する関係代名詞節。

□ open「隠し立てしない」

3 they would not 以下は，things を修飾する関係代名詞節。

第４段落

[1]An important point is the degree of exposure a person perceives. [2]Investigators in one study demonstrated that even seeing yourself reduces your sense of privacy. [3]In the experiment, participants were asked to comment either on intimate or on non-intimate topics while sitting alone in one of two small rooms and speaking into a microphone. [4]One room had bare walls; the other contained a large mirror. [5]When discussing intimate topics, participants in the mirrored room were less likely to enjoy the task, had the longest times before answering questions, gave the shortest answers, and gave less intimate information than those who couldn't see themselves. [6]Thus, the more we keep our personal details private, the more likely we are to speak our minds.

[1]重要な点は，どの程度身をさらしているのか認識することである。[2]ある調査で，研究者は自分の姿を目にするだけでプライバシーの感覚が減少することを実証した。[3]その実験では，協力者が２つの小部屋の１つに一人で座り，マイクに向かって話をする際，個人的な話題か個人的ではない話題のいずれかについて意見を述べるように求められた。[4]１つの部屋の壁には何もなくて，もう１つの部屋には大きな鏡があった。[5]個人的な話題について話しているとき，鏡のある部屋に入った協力者はその作業が楽しいと思う可能性は低く，質問に答えるまで最も時間がかかり，最も短く答え，自分の姿が見えない参加者と比べて，個人的な情報を話さなかった。[6]したがって，私的な細かいことは内密にしておけばおくほど，自分の考えを率直に話す可能性が高いのである。

1 a person perceives は exposure を修飾する関係代名詞節。

□ exposure「(身を)さらすこと，露出」　□ perceive「を認識する，知覚する」

2 □ investigator「研究者，調査者」　□ demonstrate「を実証する」　□ reduce「を減らす」

3 while sitting ... ＝while they were sitting ...　□ experiment「実験」

□ participant「協力者，参加者」　□ comment on A「Aについて意見を述べる」

□ intimate「個人的な／親密な」

4 □ bare「家具・装飾などのない」　□ contain「を含む」

5 When discussing ... ＝When they were discussing ...

those who couldn't see themselves の those は the participants の代用。

□ mirrored「鏡のある」　□ be likely to *do*「たぶん…するだろう，…する可能性が高い」
□ task「作業」
6 □ the＋比較級＋S V ...，the＋比較級＋S V 〜「…すればするほど，ますます〜する」
□ detail「詳細」　□ speak *one's* mind「自分の考えを率直に話す」

第5段落

[1]E-mail as we know it allows a high degree of privacy, which, in turn, helps generate more openness. [2]There are continuing reports from parents about e-mail communication with their children who have left home for college. [3]Sons and daughters who had little to say to their parents while still in high school, who even now rarely write or phone home, commonly e-mail just to "chat."

[1]我々が知っているようなEメールは高度なプライバシーを与えてくれ，次にそうしたプライバシーが隠し立てしなくなるのに役立つのである。[2]大学に入って実家を離れた子供とのEメールによる意思の伝達に関する親からの報告が続いている。[3]高校のときでも親と話すことがあまりなく，今でもめったに家に手紙を書いたり電話をかけてくることがない息子や娘が，ただ「おしゃべりをする」ために，Eメールを送るのはよくあることである。

3 who had little to say to their parents の little は名詞で，to say 以下は little を修飾する形容詞用法の不定詞句。
while still in high school＝while they were still in high school　□ chat「おしゃべりする」

第6段落

[1]Similarly, research on the role of computers has shown that people offer more accurate and complete information about themselves when answering questions using a computer than when answering the same questions on paper or through a face-to-face interview. [2]The differences were especially noticeable when the information at issue was personally sensitive.

[1]同様に，コンピュータの役割に関する調査では，コンピュータを使って質問に答えるときには，書面や面と向かっての面接で同じ質問に答えるときと比べて，人は自分に関するより正確で完全な情報を提供することが明らかになっている。[2]その違いは，問題になっている情報が個人的に微妙なものであるときには特に著しかった。

1 when answering ... =when they are answering ...

using a computer は answering questions と同時動作・付帯状況を表す分詞構文。

□ similarly「同様に」　□ research「研究」　□ role「役割」

2 □ noticeable「著しい，目立つ」　□ at issue「問題の」

□ sensitive「微妙な，取り扱いに慎重を要する」

5 観光と環境

解答

問1　きれいな海岸，親切な人々，そしてのんびりとした暮らし方に引かれて，1960年代中頃には，ヨーロッパのような遠く離れたところからも訪問者がその地域に大勢やって来るようになった。

問2　(2a)イ. denied that economic factors and shifting tastes were to blame
(2b)イ. produce a range of various products and services
(2c)ア. an image of a company particularly interested in environmental issues

問3　観光は世界で最も規制の少ない産業の１つであるということ。(28字)

問4　テロリズムや飛行機の旅の安全に対する恐怖が，国外旅行への関心を当分の間は減らしてしまうかもしれない。

問5　地域の資源を最大限に保護する方向に活動を変えること。

設問解説

問1　Attracted by ... of life は過去分詞で始まる分詞構文である。ここでは主節に対して，理由，補足説明を述べていると考えればよい。主節は visitors(S) began (V) coming ... (O) で，主語 visitors は from as far away as Europe の前置詞句によって修飾されており，「ヨーロッパのような遠く離れたところからの訪問者」と訳出すればよい。なお，to the region は coming を修飾していることに注意。

□ attract「を引きつける，魅了する」　□ friendly「親切な，友好的な」
□ relaxed「のんびりとした」　□ as far away as A「Aのような遠く離れたところ」
□ in large numbers「大勢で，大挙して」　□ region「地域」

問2　(2a)下線部の意味は「経済的要因と観光客の好みの変化を除外した」なので，イが正解。

ア.「経済的要因と観光客の好みの変化が主な原因であると主張した」
イ.「経済的要因と観光客の好みの変化に原因があることを否定した」
ウ.「経済的要因とゴミ処理が法律違反であるとわかった」
エ.「観光客は安くておいしい食べ物を選ぶ傾向にあるとわかった」

□ rule A out「Aを除外する」　□ factor「要因」　□ shifting「変化する」

(2b) 下線部の意味は「経済を多様化する」なので，イが正解。

ア.「数少ない主要な領域に集中する」

イ.「広範囲にわたる製品やサービスを生み出す」

ウ.「様々な多くの国と交易を始める」

エ.「経済の生産活動を厳しく管理する」

□ diversify「を多様化する」

(2c) 下線部の意味は「環境に配慮したイメージ」なので，アが正解。

ア.「特に環境問題に関心がある企業というイメージ」

イ.「ある環境に設立された企業というイメージ」

ウ.「消費者が環境を傷つけているというイメージ」

エ.「買いたいものがわかっている消費者というイメージ」

□ environmentally conscious「環境を意識した」conscious は複合語になり「…を意識した」という意味を表す。

例 class-conscious「階級意識を持った」

問 3 下線部(3)を含む文全体の意味は「このことが世界中の地域社会や文化に様々な影響を及ぼしている」である。直前の第4・5段落第3文 Tourism is ... regulated industries には「観光は世界で最も規制の少ない産業の１つである」と述べられているので，この内容が地域社会や文化に影響を及ぼしている原因であると考えられる。また，下線部を含む文の次の文には様々な影響の具体的内容が述べられている。したがって，This は第4・5段落第3文を制限字数内にまとめればよい。

問 4 全体の構造は，Fears of terrorism and the safety of air travel(S) may have lessened(V) interest in some international travel(O) である。また，and が結んでいるのが terrorism と the safety of air travel であることにも注意。Fears of terrorism と the safety of air travel を結んでいると考えると，文意が通じない。なお，for the time being が「当分の間は」という意味であることと，続く文の内容から，may have *done* がここでは「…してしまうかもしれない」という意味であり，よく用いられる「…したかもしれない」ではないことにも注意。

例 1 By next week, they may have completed their contract.
「来週までには彼らは契約を結んでしまうかもしれない」

例 2 They may already have completed their contract.
「彼らはすでに契約を結んでしまったかもしれない」

□ fear of A「Aへの恐怖(感)」　□ terrorism「テロリズム」

□ air travel「飛行機の旅」　□ lessen「を減らす」　□ interest in A「Aに対する関心」

問5 下線部(5)を含む文全体の意味は「これは責任ある観光の範囲をはるかに越える根本的な変化を必要とする」である。直前の第7段落第1文には,「観光の影響が良くも悪くも広がり続けるにつれて,その地域の資源を最大限に保護する方向に活動を変えることがますます重要になる」と述べられており,「変化が必要とされること」について言及されている。また,続く第3文の「その変化について具体的にあらゆるレベルで人が関わることが必要である」は,下線部を含む文の補足説明となっている。したがって,第1文の to redirect ... the fullest をまとめればよい。

Advice 内容説明問題① 指示語 this

指示語 this の具体的内容を問う問題で,this の指している部分は以下の3つである。

1．直前の文全体および複数の文の内容

例 He got into the habit of drinking every day. This was his downfall.

「彼は毎日酒を飲むようになった。これ(＝彼が毎日酒を飲むようになったこと)が彼の破滅のもとであった」

2．直前の文の一部の内容

例 In the sixteenth century it was believed that the earth was the center of the universe. We know this is not true.

「16世紀には,地球が宇宙の中心であると信じられていた。私たちはこれ(＝地球が宇宙の中心であること)が本当ではないと知っている」

3．直後の文の内容

例 I'll say this: she's strictly honest.

「言っておくが,彼女はまったく正直だ」

指示語の内容説明問題においては,与えられた制限字数がヒントになることも多い。また,指示内容を指示語に当てはめて文脈が自然につながれば,正しいことが確認できる。

要 約

インドの漁村コバラムに見られるように,近年,観光地におけるゴミ問題をはじめとした自然破壊が問題になっている。環境や文化の保護と地域経済の発展の両立を可能にする観光事業が求められている。(92字)

▶▶▶ 構文・語句解説 ◀◀◀

第1段落

[1]Until recently, Kovalam, a small fishing village in India's Kerala state, could not keep up with its rising popularity. [2]Attracted by clean beaches, friendly people and a relaxed way of life, visitors from as far away as Europe began coming in large numbers to the region in the mid-1960s. [3]Over the next two decades, investors rushed in to meet the demand, building row upon row of new hotels, restaurants and souvenir shops. [4]But in 1993 the tourist stream began to slow. [5]By 2000, the number of tourists had decreased by 40 percent.

[1]最近まで，インドのケララ州の小さな漁村コバラムは人気の高まりについていくことができなかった。[2]きれいな海岸，親切な人々，そしてのんびりとした暮らし方に引かれて，1960年代中頃には，ヨーロッパのような遠く離れたところからも訪問者がその地域に大勢やって来るようになった。[3]その後20年間にわたり，需要を満たすために投資家たちがなだれ込んできて，次々と新しいホテルやレストランや土産物店を建てた。[4]しかし，1993年に観光客の流れは鈍くなり始めた。[5]2000年までには観光客の数は40%も落ち込んでいた。

1 Kovalam と a small fishing village in India's Kerala state は同格の関係。

□ keep up with A「Aに遅れずについていく」

3 building row upon ... shops は連続・結果を表す分詞構文。

row upon row of ... とは次々とホテルやレストランが建てられていったことを表している。

□ decade「10年間」　□ investor「投資家」　□ rush in「なだれ込む」

□ meet the demand「需要を満たす」　□ row「〈人や物の〉列」

□ souvenir shop「土産物店」

4 □ stream「流れ」

5 □ the number of A「Aの数」　□ by A「Aだけ，Aの分」差を表す。

第2・3段落

[1]Travel experts ruled out economic factors and shifting tourist tastes, finally explaining the decline as one caused by the community's waste management problems. [2]Like many popular destinations in the developing world, Kovalam has no formal plan to deal with the growing levels of garbage generated by tourists. [3]Hotels and other facilities collect recyclable items, such as glass, paper and metal scraps, for reuse by local industries whenever possible. [4]The less desirable items — plastic bottles and even uneaten food, for

example — simply pile up in towering mounds or are dumped into nearby streams, posing the risk of serious disease.

[5]Yet, a local politician complained, “Nobody bothers about the health issues faced by people. [6]Everybody wants Kovalam beach to be clean just so it can get more business.”

[1]旅行関係の専門家は，経済的要因や観光客の好みの変化を除外し，その低迷は村のゴミ処理問題によるものだと最終的に説明した。[2]発展途上諸国の多くの人気のある観光地と同様に，コバラムは観光客の出すどんどん増えるゴミを処理するきちんとした計画を持っていない。[3]ホテルやその他の施設は，ガラス，紙，金属くずなどのリサイクル可能なものを地域の産業が再使用できるときは集めている。[4]たとえばペットボトルや食べ残しのようなそれほど歓迎されないものは，ただ山のように積み上げられるか近くの川に投棄され，深刻な病気が発生する危険が生じている。

[5]しかし，地元の政治家が不満を述べた。「人々が直面している健康の問題などには誰も関心を持っていません。[6]みんなもっと商売になるようにコバラムの海岸がきれいになってほしいだけなのです」

1 finally explaining ... management problems は分詞構文。caused by 以下は one を修飾する過去分詞句で，one は a decline の代用。 □ expert「専門家」 □ explain「を説明する」 □ decline「低迷，衰退」 □ cause「を引き起こす」 □ community「地域社会」 □ waste「ゴミ，廃棄物」 □ management「管理」

2 □ destination「目的地」 □ formal「正式な」 □ deal with A「Aを処理する」 □ garbage「ゴミ」 □ generate「を生み出す」

3 □ facilities「施設」 □ recyclable「再利用できる，リサイクルできる」 □ item「品目」 □ metal scrap「金属くず」 □ reuse「再利用」 □ local「地元の」 □ industry「産業」 □ whenever possible「可能なときはいつでも」

4 posing the ... serious disease は連続・結果を表す分詞構文。 □ desirable「望ましい」 □ pile up「積み重なる」 □ towering「高くそびえる」 □ mound「小山」 □ dump「を捨てる」 □ nearby「近くの」 □ pose「を引き起こす」

5 □ bother about A「Aを心配する」 □ issue「問題」 □ face「に直面する」

6 □ just so it can get more business は so that S can *do*「Sが…するために」という目的を表す構文を用いたもので，that が省略されている。なお，just は so 以下を強調している。

第４・５段落

[1]These problems are not unique to Kovalam. [2]Increasingly, developing countries are turning to tourism as a way to diversify their economies, stimulate investments and create earnings.

[3]Tourism is one of the world's least regulated industries. [4]This has implications for communities and cultures around the world. [5]Hotels, tourist transport and related activities consume huge amounts of energy, water and other resources; and they produce pollution, often in destinations that are unprepared to deal with these impacts. [6]In addition, many communities face cultural troubles and other unwelcome changes that accompany higher visitor numbers. [7]Fears of terrorism and the safety of air travel may have lessened interest in some international travel for the time being. [8]However, over the long term the demand for tourism is expected to resume its steady rise.

[1]これらの問題はコバラムだけのものではない。[2]発展途上国は経済を多様化し，投資を刺激し，利益を創出する一手段としてますます観光事業に目を向けている。

[3]観光事業は世界で最も規制の少ない産業の１つである。[4]このことが世界中の地域社会や文化に様々な影響を及ぼしている。[5]ホテルや観光客輸送や関連活動は膨大な量のエネルギー，水，その他の資源を消費する。そしてこれらの活動はこうした影響に対処する用意の整っていない場所でしばしば公害を引き起こす。[6]そのうえ，多くの共同体が観光客が増えるのに伴って起こる文化的な問題やその他の歓迎されない変化に直面する。[7]テロリズムや飛行機の旅の安全に対する恐怖が，国外旅行への関心を当分の間は減らしてしまうかもしれない。[8]しかし，長期的には観光客の需要は再び安定した増加を始めると予想されている。

1 □ unique to A「Aに特異な，独特な」

2 □ increasingly「ますます」　□ turn to A「Aに目を向ける」　□ tourism「観光事業」

□ stimulate「を刺激する」　□ investment「投資」　□ earnings「〈企業の〉利益，事業所得」

3 □ regulated「規制された」

4 □ implication「影響」

5 □ transport「輸送」　□ related「関連した」　□ consume「を消費する」

□ resources「資源」　□ pollution「公害，汚染」

□ be unprepared to *do*「…する用意ができていない」　□ impact「影響」

6 □ in addition「そのうえ」　□ accompany「に伴って起こる」

8 □ term「期間」　□ be expected to *do*「…すると予想されている」　□ resume「を始める」

第6段落

[1]Many governments, industry groups and others are promoting responsible travel that makes money and creates jobs while also protecting the local environments and cultures. [2]While it does succeed in some circumstances, this kind of environmentally responsible tourism can produce many of the same problems as ordinary tourism, including the creation of waste. [3]In some cases it is little more than a marketing tool for businesses hoping to promote an environmentally conscious image.

[1]多くの政府，業界団体などは，お金が儲かり仕事も創出する一方で，その地域の環境や文化を保護する，責任ある旅行を促進している。[2]ある状況ではうまくいっても，このような環境に責任を持つ観光もふつうの観光と同じように，ゴミの産出も含めて多くの問題を生む可能性がある。[3]環境意識が高いというイメージを売り込みたい企業にとっては，それはマーケティング手段くらいのものでしかない場合もある。

1 that makes ... and cultures は responsible travel を修飾する関係代名詞節。while は対比を表し，while の後には it is が省略されている。

□ industry group「業界団体」　□ promote「を促進する」　□ responsible「責任のある」

2 does succeed の does は動詞強調の助動詞。

can produce ... の can は可能性を表し，「…することもある」という意味。

□ circumstance「状況」　□ including A「Aを含めて」

3 it は this kind of environmentally responsible tourism を指している。

□ little more than A「Aにすぎない，Aと大差ない」

第7段落

[1]As tourism's impacts, both good and bad, continue to spread, it is more and more important to redirect activities onto a path that protects local resources to the fullest. [2]This will require deep changes that reach far beyond the scope of responsible tourism. [3]A broad range of people and organizations, including executives at large companies, governments, nongovernmental groups and the tourists themselves, will need to become involved with the efforts to protect and maintain, at all levels, the environment and culture of the various places to which tourists go.

[1]観光の影響が良くも悪くも広がり続けるにつれて，その地域の資源を最大限に保護する方向に活動を変えることがますます重要になる。[2]これは責任ある観光の範囲をはるかに越える根本的な変化を必要とする。[3]大企業の経営陣，政府，非政府組織そして観光客自身を含む広範な人材と組織が，観光客が訪れる様々な土地の環境や文化をあらゆるレベルで守り維持する努力に関わることが必要である。

1 both good and bad は tourism's impacts を補足説明している。　□ spread「広がる」
□ redirect「の方向を変える」　□ to the fullest「最大限に」

2 □ beyond A「A（の範囲）を越えて」　□ scope「範囲」

3 the environment and culture は protect と maintain の共通の目的語である。
to which tourists go は the various places を修飾する関係代名詞節。
□ range「範囲」
□ executive「〈企業などの〉経営者[陣]，重役」　□ nongovernmental「非政府の，民間の」
□ become involved with A「Aに関わるようになる」　□ effort to *do*「…しようとする努力」

6 視覚と認識

解　答

問1　私たちは，目が教えてくれるものがいったい何なのか，本当にそんなに確信が持てるのだろうか。

問2　if we had not read what astronomers tell us

問3　結局のところ，私たちは，見るものを信じるというよりはむしろ，信じるものを見るのである。

問4　brain

問5　the images

問6　脳が学習したことはどのように私たちが「物を見る」と呼ぶ過程に影響しているのかを示す例を，あといくつか挙げてみたい。

問7　(7a) ウ．near　(7b) エ．further away　(7c) ア．large
(7d) イ．tiny

問8　size

▶▶▶ 設問解説 ◀◀◀

問1　文全体は，be sure wh-節「〈否定文・疑問文で〉…について確信している」の wh-節に what it is that ... という疑問詞 what を強調する強調構文の間接疑問が入った形。what it is that ... は「…はいったい何なのか」と訳出するとよい。なお，what は tell O_1 O_2「O_1〈人〉に O_2〈事〉を話す」の O_2 に当たる。

例　What is it that my daughter wants for her birthday?
「娘が誕生日に欲しがっているのはいったい何だろう」

問2　文頭の Could と選択肢の if から，全体が仮定法の文で，下線部がその条件節となっていることが予想できる。条件節内の主語としては astronomers，we または what 節が考えられるが，この文の主節および第1段落からの意味の流れから，we を主語にして had not read を述語とし，関係代名詞 what が導く節を目的語として，「もし私たちが天文学者が私たちに教えてくれるものを読んだことがなければ」という意味にすれば，主節が表す意味にも自然につながる。なお，条件節が仮定法過去完了，帰結節が仮定法過去になっていることに注意。

□ astronomer「天文学者」　□ tell A about B「AにBのことを教える」

問3 全体の文構造は What it amounts to(S) is(V) that ...(C) であり，「結局のところ，…だ」という意味の慣用表現である。that 以下には not so much X as Y「XというよりむしろY」の表現が用いられており，X が believe what we see，Y が see what we believe となっている。なお，この下線部の what は，いずれも関係代名詞であることに注意。

問4 空所(4)を含む文は「見ることは目の活動であるばかりではなく(　4　)の活動でもあり，それは一種の選択機械として機能している」という意味。第3段落全体が「脳が網膜上の像をどのように処理するか」を説明していることから空所(4)に brain を入れると，自然な文意になる。

問5 下線部(5)を含む文全体は choose A out of B「BからAを選ぶ」の out of B が文頭に出て，Aに当たる those that ... past experience の前に for recognition「認識のために」という前置詞句が挿入された形になっている。したがって，文全体は「脳に提示されるすべての像の中から，過去の経験によって学習した世界に最もよく合う those を脳は認識のために選ぶのである」という意味になる。「すべての像の中から those を選ぶ」という関係に注目すれば，those が「像」を指すことがわかる。

問6 to show ... は examples を修飾する形容詞用法の不定詞句。show の目的語は how以下の疑問詞節で，その節内はwhat the brain has learned(S) influences(V) the process we call “seeing things”(O) という構造になっている。we call “seeing things” は the process を修飾する関係代名詞節。

□ influence「に影響を与える」　□ process「過程，プロセス」

問7 第4段落では「物が何も置かれていない廊下に白い紙やトランプを置き，のぞき穴を通して見た結果，その距離や大きさを当てる」という設定の中で，その紙やトランプに関する情報を言葉で伝えられると，脳が学習したことに影響されて答えが左右される様子が述べられている。

(7a) (7b) 白い紙が「名刺」であると教えられる場合と，「大きな封筒」であると教えられる場合，紙が同じ大きさに見える限り，名刺の場合なら「近くにある(near)」ように思えるはずであり，大きな封筒の場合には「より遠くにある(further away)」ように思えるはずである。

(7c) (7d) トランプを見せられる場合，トランプの大きさはたいていの場合同じであるという思いこみがあるため，「大きな(large)トランプ」を見せられると近くにあるように思えるはずであり，「小さな(tiny)トランプ」を見せられると遠くにあるように思えるはずである。

ア.「大きい」 イ.「小さい」 ウ.「近い」 エ.「より遠い」

問8 「物の『大きさ』を目だけからの情報ではなく，その物に関する様々な情報を総合して脳が判断している」という第4段落全体の内容から，空所には size を入れるのが自然である。

Advice 内容説明問題② 指示語 that

指示語 that は，this 同様，**直前の文および複数の文の内容や前の文の一部の内容**を指す。ただし，this とは異なり直後の文の内容を指すことはない。また，前述の名詞の反復を避けるために，**the + 名詞の代用**となり，修飾語を伴って用いられる。なお，**the + 複数形の名詞の代用**となる場合は those が用いられる。

例1 The climate of Japan is milder than that of England.
「日本の気候はイギリスのそれ(＝気候)よりも温暖である」

例2 The mountains of Greece are less thickly wooded than those of England.
「ギリシアの山はイギリスのそれ(＝山)より木が少ない」

要約

自分の目で見たものは確かだ，と信じている人が多いが，実際には，脳が学習した情報や周囲の状況から得られる情報が物の見え方に多大な影響を与えているのである。(76字)

構文・語句解説

第1段落

1How often do we say "Of course I believe it—I saw it with my own eyes!" 2But can we really be so sure what it is that our eyes tell us? 3For example, take the simple question, "How big is the moon?"

1私たちはどれくらい頻繁に「もちろんそれを信じているよ。自分の目で見たんだから！」と言うことだろう。2しかし，私たちは，目が教えてくれるものがいったい何なのか，本当にそんなに確信が持てるのだろうか。3たとえば，「月はどれくらいの大きさか」という単純な質問を取り上げてみよう。

1 □ how often ...「どれくらいの頻度で…」

3 □ take「を例として取り上げる」

第2段落

[1]Could any of us make a good estimate of the moon's size if we had not read what astronomers tell us about its diameter? [2]What does looking at the moon, or any other object, tell us about its real size? [3]What do we mean by "real" size or "real" shape, or other appearance, for that matter? [4]Can we believe what we see of things; or rather, putting it the other way round, what do we mean when we say we believe that a thing has a certain size or shape?

[1]月の直径について天文学者が教えてくれることを読んだことがなければ，私たちのうちの誰が月の大きさに関して適切な推測を行うことができるであろうか。[2]月，あるいは他のどんな物であれ，それを目にすることで，その本当の大きさについて何がわかるのだろうか。[3]もっと言えば，「本当の」大きさや「本当の」形，あるいはその他の目に映るものというとき，私たちは何を言おうとしているのだろう。[4]私たちは物に関して目にするものを信じることができるのだろうか？というよりは，逆に言えば，ある物がある大きさや形を持っていると信じると言うときに，私たちは何を言おうとしているのだろう。

1 □ make a good estimate of A「Aに関して適切な推測を行う」　□ diameter「直径」

2 動名詞句 looking at the moon, or any other object が主語となっている。　□ object「物」

3 □ mean A by B「Bという表現でAを意味する」　□ appearance「外見，見かけ」

□ for that matter「もっと言えば，さらに詳しく言えば」

4 putting it the other way round「逆に言えば」は慣用的な分詞構文。

□ or rather「〈前言を言い直して〉もっと正確に言えば，というよりはむしろ」

□ certain A「あるA」

第3段落

[1]The brain interprets the image on the retina in the light of all sorts of other "information" it receives. [2]Perception, in fact, is by no means a simple recording of the details of the world seen outside. [3]It is a selection of those features with which we are familiar. [4]What it amounts to is that we do not so much believe what we see as see what we believe. [5]Seeing is an activity not only of our eyes but of the brain, which works as a sort of selecting machine. [6]Out of all the images presented to it, it chooses for recognition those that fit most closely with the world learned by past experience.

[1]脳は網膜上の像を，脳が受け取るあらゆる種類の他の「情報」に照らし合わせて解釈する。[2]実は，知覚とは外に見える世界の細部を単に記録することでは決してない。[3]それは私たちがよく知っている特徴を選択することなのである。[4]結局のところ，私たちは，見るものを信じるというよりはむしろ，信じるものを見るのである。[5]見ることは目の活動であるばかりでなく脳の活動でもあり，脳は一種の選択機械として機能している。[6]脳に提示されるすべての像の中から，過去の経験によって学習した世界に最もよく合うものを脳は認識のために選ぶのである。

1 it receives は other "information" を修飾する関係代名詞節。 □ interpret「を解釈する」
□ image「像，映像」 □ in (the) light of A「Aに照らし合わせて，Aを考慮して」
□ sort「種類」

2 □ perception「知覚」 □ in fact「実際，実は」 □ by no means「決して…でない」
□ recording「記録すること」 □ detail「細部，詳細」

3 those は with which 以下の関係代名詞節が修飾する語を明示している。 □ selection「選択」
□ feature「特徴」 □ be familiar with A「Aをよく知っている，Aに詳しい」

5 □ not only X but Y「XだけでなくYも」 □ work as A「Aとして機能する」
□ selecting machine「選択するための機械」

6 □ present A to B「AをBに提示する」 □ recognition「認識」
□ fit with A「Aに一致する，合う」 □ closely「ぴったりと」

第4段落

[1]I want to give a few more examples to show how what the brain has learned influences the process we call "seeing things." [2]Seeing, they say, is believing. [3]But is it? [4]An arrangement can be made in such a way that a person looks through a peephole into a bare corridor, so bare that it gives no clues about distance. [5]If you now show him a piece of white paper in the corridor and ask how large it is, his reply will be influenced by any suggestion you make as to what the piece of paper may be. [6]If you tell him that the particular piece of paper is a business card, he will say that it is quite near. [7]Show him the piece of paper at the same distance and tell him that it is a large envelope, and he will say that it is further away. [8]On the other hand, if you show a very large playing card, say a Queen of Spades, he will say that it is very close, and if you show a tiny one he will say it is a long way away, because, you see, playing cards are nearly always of a standard size. [9]In fact, the size of things we perceive depends upon what we otherwise know about them. [10]When we see a car from far away, its image on the retina is no

bigger than that of a toy seen near, but we take the surroundings into consideration and give its proper size.

[1]脳が学習したことはどのように私たちが「物を見る」と呼ぶ過程に影響しているのかを示す例を，あといくつか挙げてみたい。[2]見ることは信じることだと言われている。[3]しかし，そうなのだろうか？[4]物が置かれていないので距離に関する手がかりがまったく得られない廊下を，のぞき穴を通して見ることができるように準備することができる。[5]もしその廊下に１枚の白い紙を置いて見せ，どれくらいの大きさかを尋ねると，その答えは紙が何であるかについて与えられるいかなるヒントにも影響を受けるだろう。[6]もしその特定の紙が名刺であると言えば，かなり近くにある，と言うであろう。[7]同じ距離にその紙を置いて見せ，それは大きな封筒だと言うと，それはもっと遠くにある，と言うだろう。[8]一方，とても大きなトランプを，仮にスペードのクイーンを見せると，とても近いところにあると言うだろうし，とても小さなトランプを見せると，遠くにあると言うであろう。というのは，知っての通りトランプはほとんどいつでも標準的なサイズだからである。[9]実際，私たちが知覚する物の大きさは，他の点で私たちがそれらに関して知っていることに左右される。[10]遠くから来る車を見るとき，網膜上のその像は近くに見えるおもちゃほどの大きさしかないのだが，私たちは周りの状況を考慮に入れてその正しい大きさを判断するのである。

2 Seeing, they say, is believing. = They say that seeing is believing.　Seeing is believing. は通例「百聞は一見にしかず」という意味のことわざ。

4 so bare 以下は a bare corridor を補足説明している。so ... that ～は「～するほど…／あまりに…なので～」という意味。　□ make an arrangement「準備をする，手配する」
□ in such a way that節「…するように」
□ look through A into B「Aを通してBの中を見る」　□ peephole「のぞき穴」
□ bare「〈場所などに〉物がない」　□ corridor「廊下」　□ clue「手がかり，ヒント」
□ distance「距離」

5 you make ... may be は any suggestion を修飾する関係代名詞節。
□ suggestion「ほのめかし，ヒント」　□ as to A「Aに関して」

6 □ business card「名刺」

7 命令文, and S V ...「～しなさい，そうすれば…」の表現で，Show him ... same distance と tell him ... large envelope が and で結ばれている。　□ envelope「封筒」

8 □ on the other hand「ところが一方」　□ playing card「トランプ」　□ say「たとえば」
□ close「近い」　□ a long way away「遠く離れて」
□ you see「知ってのとおり，おわかりでしょうが」　□ be of a ... size「…な大きさである」

□ standard「標準的な」

9 we perceive は things を修飾する関係代名詞節。　□ perceive「を知覚する」

□ depend upon A「Aに左右される，A次第である」　□ otherwise「その他の点で」

10 that は the image の代用。　□ from far away「遠くから」

□ no bigger than A「Aの大きさにすぎない，Aと同じほど小さい」

□ take A into consideration「Aを考慮に入れる」　□ surroundings「周囲の状況，環境」

□ proper「正しい」

7 気象制御

解答

問1 自然の脅威や大災害を原因とする人的，経済的両面の損失を減らし，経済面でさらには軍事面で隣国より優位に立ちたいため。(57字)

問2 自然の脅威それ自体を変える方法とその影響を減らす方法の組み合わせ。(33字)

問3 releases about 100,000 times as much energy as did

問4 ウ. without

問5 気象改変計画は，うまくいっても失敗しても，この分野での大規模な活動の見通しをきわめて不確かなものにする様々な問題をもたらすことになる。

問6 不利益が利益よりも大きくなるようなカテゴリー。(23字)

問7 ア. Nor does it stop there.

設問解説

問1 下線部は「気象改変」という意味。第2段落第1文の前半に「気象を変えようとするもっともな理由が1つある」とあり，続いて「それ(＝気象を変えようとするもっともな理由)は，自然の脅威や大災害を原因とする人的，経済的両面の損失を減らすことである」と述べられているので，理由の1つは「自然の脅威や大災害を原因とする人的，経済的両面の損失を減らすこと」である。また，第2段落第2文に，「他にも理由はある」とあり，続いて「その(＝他の理由)中には，経済面でさらには軍事面で隣国より優位に立ちたいという願望も含まれるかもしれない」と述べられているので，他の理由が「経済面でさらには軍事面で隣国より優位に立つこと」である。したがって，これらの理由をまとめればよい。

□ modification「改変，修正」

問2 下線部(2)を含む文は，「これら2つの方法は，互いに相容れないものである必要はなく，場合によっては組み合わせることで最良の結果が得られることもある」という意味であり，下線部の「組み合わせ」とは，These two methods「これら2つの方法」の組み合わせであると考えられる。These two methods は，第2段落第3文の「そうした(＝自然の)脅威それ自体を変えること」と「その影響を減らすこと」を指しているので，この2つをまとめればよい。

□ combination「組み合わせ」

問 3 下線部(3)を含む文は，To illustrate this「これを説明するために」から始まり，this は前の文「大気の破壊力は，人間がそれに及ぼす制御力をはるかに超えている」を指しているので，下線部を含む部分が，「大西洋や太平洋上に発生する典型的な冬の嵐が，最初の原子爆弾よりも多くのエネルギーを放出する」という内容になるように並べ換えればよい。X times as＋原級＋as ...「…のX倍～」の X に about 100,000 を置いて，releases about 100,000 times as much energy as とすれば，「…の約10万倍のエネルギーを放出する」となり「より多くのエネルギーを放出する」という意味が表現できる。なお，releases energy about 100,000 times as much as と並べ換えるのは，前提となる release energy much という表現がないので，不可。また，比較対象を表す２つめの as 以下では倒置が生じることがあるので，最後に did を置けばよい。

例 This towel absorbs three times as much water as does a common cotton towel.

「このタオルは，普通のコットンのタオルの３倍水を吸収する」

□ release「を放出する」

問 4 空所(4)を含む文は，前に述べたことが原因となって結果として生じることを述べるときに用いられる Thus「したがって」から始まっており，直前の文には「大気への干渉は，大気が２つの対照的な状態の間でうまくバランスがとれている場合のように，うまくいく特定の状況がある」ことが述べられている。したがって，without を入れれば，「雨を降らせるための雲の種まき作戦は，雲が発達する良好な条件がなければ決してうまくいかないが，厚い雲の発達がすでに進行しているなら，成功するかもしれない」となり，文脈が自然なつながりとなる。なお，cloud-seeding「雲の種まき」とは，雲に直接ヨウ化銀やドライアイスといった化学物質をまくことで，水蒸気が集まる核を人工的に作り，雲が持つ潜在的降水量を最大限に引き出す技術のこと。

問 5 whether successful or not「うまくいっても失敗しても」が主語と動詞の間に挿入されている。whether の後ろに they(＝weather modification projects) are を補って考えることができるが，whether X or Y が挿入で用いられている場合は，「Xであろうと Yであろうと」と意味を取ればよい。

例 She is always cheerful, whether sick or well.

「彼女は調子が悪くてもよくても，いつも明るい」

which 以下は a variety of problems を修飾する関係代名詞節。節内では the prospect of large-scale activity in this field が make O C「OをCにする」の O になっている。

□ a variety of A「様々なA」　□ prospect「見通し」　□ large-scale「大規模な」
□ activity「活動」　□ field「分野」　□ uncertain「不確かな」

問6 下線部(6)を含む文は，「霧とか雲を散らすために大量の熱エネルギーを放出したり，嵐を弱体化するために広範囲に電場を作り出したりすることも同じようなカテゴリーに分類できる」という意味。直前の文に「雲の種まきに使われる化学物質のほとんどが大気汚染の原因となり，これらの不利益は種まきの過程で得られる利益よりも大きいかもしれないのだ」とあるので，「同じようなカテゴリー」とは，「不利益が利益よりも大きくなるようなカテゴリー」であると考えられる。

□ category「カテゴリー，範疇」

問7 空所(7)の前の第4段落第4～6文では，「気象改変の影響は意図された地域に制限することができない」と述べられている。空所の後ろの第5段落では，「ハリケーンや台風が邪魔されると，世界規模で連鎖反応が起きるかもしれない」と述べられている。したがって，アが正解。なお nor「また…でない」は，後ろに S V ... がくると必ず倒置が起きる。it は「気象改変の影響」というここでの話題を指している。

ア.「話はそこで終わらない」
イ.「話はそこでようやく終わる」
ウ.「それで，それが常に実情である」
エ.「したがって，それが実情ではない」

Advice 内容説明問題③　the same / similar / opposite

特に2つのものを挙げてその対比および比較を軸に論旨が展開する場合，the same「同じ(こと)」や similar「同様の」, opposite「正反対の(こと)」などの内容を問う問題が出題されることが多い。このような問題の場合，対比・比較されているものが何であるのかを押さえた上で，前に述べられた内容から「同じ，同様の」こと，あるいは「正反対の」ことが何であるのかを考える必要がある。本問の問6では，a similar category の similar が何に対して「同様の」ことなのかが問われている。

要　約

自然の脅威とその影響を減らすために気象制御の試みが行われている。しかし，気象制御は良好な条件がないと難しく，利益よりも不利益の方が大きく，その結果起きるかもしれない連鎖反応も不明である。(93字)

構文・語句解説

第1段落

[1]We have all had moments when we would have liked to switch on the sunshine or switch off the rain, or to affect the outdoor temperature. [2]Ever since early humans set up home in the nearest cave, or lit the first fire, we have tried to adjust the climate surrounding us—you could call these the first attempts at weather control. [3]Today, weather control might be thought of as a fantasy world for crazy scientists, but there are some kinds of weather modification—though few in number—which are routine in certain areas of human activity.

[1]日光のスイッチを入れたり，雨のスイッチを切ったり，あるいは戸外の温度を変えたりしたいとふと思ったことは誰しもある。[2]原始人が最も近くにある洞穴に住まいを構えたときか，あるいは初めて火を起こしたとき以来，我々は周囲の気候を調節しようとしてきた—これを気象制御の最初の試みと呼べるだろう。[3]今日，気象制御は頭のおかしい科学者の空想の世界と考えられるかもしれないが，人間の活動の特定分野で日常的に行われているある種の気象改変は—数は少ないが—存在する。

1 all は We と同格の関係。when 以下は moments を修飾する関係副詞節。1つめの or は switch on the sunshine と switch off the rain を，2つめの or は to switch ... the rain と，to affect the outdoor temperature を結んでいる。

□would have liked to *do*「…したかった」　□switch A on「Aのスイッチを入れる」

□switch A off「Aのスイッチを切る」　□affect「に影響を与える」

□outdoor「屋外の」　□temperature「気温」

2 or は set up home in the nearest cave と lit the first fire の2つの動詞句を結んでいる。surrounding us は the climate を修飾する現在分詞句。

□early humans「原始人，初期の人類」　□set up home「家を構える」

□cave「洞窟」　□lit<light「火をつける，灯す」の過去形。

□try to *do*「…しようとする」　□adjust「を調節する」　□climate「天候」

□call O C「OをCと呼ぶ」　□attempt at A「Aしようという試み」

□weather control「気象制御」

3 which 以下は some kinds of weather modification を修飾する関係代名詞節。

□think of O as C「OをCと考える」　□fantasy world「空想の世界」

□though few in number「数は少ないが」　□routine「決まってすること」

□certain A「あるA」　□human「人間の」

第2段落

[1]There is one powerful reason to seek to alter the weather, and that is to reduce the losses, both human and economic, caused by a natural hazard or disaster. [2]There are other reasons but these do not have the same moral force: they may include a desire for economic or even military advantage over a neighbor. [3]Saving human lives and property can be achieved either by modifying the hazard itself or by reducing its impact. [4]These two methods need not be mutually exclusive, and in certain cases a combination may provide the best results. [5]Insurance may also help to soften the blow of damaged property or loss of earnings.

[1]気象を変えようとするもっともな理由が1つあるが，それは，自然の脅威や大災害を原因とする人的，経済的両面の損失を減らすことである。[2]他にも理由はあるが，これらには同じような道義的説得力はない。その中には，経済面でさらには軍事面で隣国より優位に立ちたいという願望も含まれるかもしれない。[3]そうした脅威それ自体を変えることか，その影響を減らすことによって，人命や財産を守ることはできる。[4]これら2つの方法は，互いに相容れないものである必要はなく，場合によっては組み合わせることで最良の結果が得られることもある。[5]また，保険が被害を受けた財産や所得の損失の打撃を軽減するのに役立つこともある。

1 both human and economic は the losses を補足説明する形容詞句。caused 以下は the losses を修飾する過去分詞句。

□ reason to *do*「…する理由」　□ seek to *do*「…しようと努める」　□ alter「を変える」
□ reduce「を減らす」　□ loss「損失」　□ both X and Y「XとYの両方」
□ economic「経済の」　□ cause「の原因となる，を引き起こす」
□ hazard「脅威，危険を引き起こすもの」　□ disaster「大災害，災難」

2 or は economic と even military の2つの形容詞(句)を結んでいる。

□ moral「道義上の，道徳的な」　□ force「力」　□ include「を含む」
□ desire for A「Aに対する願望」　□ military「軍事の」
□ advantage over A「Aより有利な点」　□ neighbor「隣国，隣人」

3 and は，saving の目的語である2つの名詞(句) human lives と property を結んでいる。

□ save「を守る，救う」　□ property「財産，資産」　□ achieve「を達成する」
□ either X or Y「XかYのいずれか」　□ modify「を変える，修正する」
□ impact「影響」

4 □ method「方法」　□ mutually「相互に」　□ exclusive「相容れない，排他的な」

☐ case「場合」　☐ provide「を提供する」

5 ☐ insurance「保険」　☐ help to *do*「…するのに役立つ」

☐ soften「を軽減する，和らげる」　☐ blow「打撃」　☐ damaged「被害を受けた」

☐ earnings「所得」

第3段落

[1]Weather disasters are generally more difficult to control than terrible events such as landslides where large-scale engineering projects can reduce the frequency and the magnitude of the hazard. [2]The destructive forces of the atmosphere, however, far exceed how much control human beings have over them. [3]To illustrate this we can make a rough estimate that a typical winter storm over the Atlantic or Pacific releases about 100,000 times as much energy as did the first atomic bomb. [4]Even if we wanted to interfere with the atmosphere on this scale, the analysis of costs versus benefits would soon see the project cancelled. [5]There are, though, certain circumstances when intervention can work: when the atmosphere is finely balanced between two contrasting states, we can successfully change that balance with relatively little cost and effort. [6]Thus cloud-seeding operations to create rain will never work without favorable conditions for the development of clouds, but they may succeed if deep cloud development is already occurring.

[1]気象による災害は，地滑りのような恐ろしい出来事よりも，一般的には制御が難しい。そのような出来事の場合，大規模土木事業でその脅威の頻度や度合いを減らすことができる。[2]しかし，大気の破壊力は，人間がそれに及ぼす制御力をはるかに超えている。[3]これを説明するために，我々は，大西洋や太平洋上に発生する典型的な冬の嵐が，最初の原子爆弾の約10万倍のエネルギーを放出するという概算を行うことができる。[4]この規模で大気に干渉したくても，費用便益分析を行えば，そんな計画は放棄されてしまうとすぐにわかるだろう。[5]しかし，大気への干渉がうまくいく特定の状況がある。たとえば，大気が2つの対照的な状態の間でうまくバランスがとれている場合は，比較的小さなコストと労力でそのバランスを首尾よく変えることができる。[6]したがって，雨を降らせるための雲の種まき作戦は，雲が発達する良好な条件がなければ決してうまくいかないが，厚い雲の発達がすでに進行しているなら，成功するかもしれない。

1 where 以下は terrible events を修飾する関係副詞節。and は the frequency と the magnitude の2つの名詞句を結んでいる。

□ be difficult to *do*「…するのが難しい」 □ generally「一般的に」
□ terrible「恐ろしい」 □ A such as B「たとえばBのようなA」 □ landslide「地滑り」
□ engineering project「土木事業」 □ frequency「頻度」 □ magnitude「度合い，規模」

2 □ destructive「破壊的な」 □ the atmosphere「大気」 □ exceed「を超える」
□ control over A「Aに対する制御(力)，支配」

3 □ illustrate「を説明する，例証する」 □ make an estimate that 節「…であると見積もる」
□ rough「大まかな」 □ typical「典型的な」 □ storm「嵐」 □ the Atlantic「大西洋」
□ the Pacific「太平洋」 □ atomic bomb「原子爆弾」

4 □ interfere with A「Aに干渉する，を邪魔する」 □ on this scale「この規模で」
□ analysis「分析」 □ A versus B「Bに対してA，A対B」 □ benefit「便益，利益」
□ see O *done*「Oが…されるのが見える」 □ cancel「を取り消す，無効にする」

5 when intervention can work は certain circumstances を修飾する関係副詞節。
□ though「しかし，もっとも」 □ circumstances「状況」 □ intervention「干渉，介入」
□ work「うまくいく」 □ be balanced between A「Aの間でバランスがとれている」
□ finely「うまく，見事に」 □ contrasting「対照的な」 □ state「状態」
□ relatively「比較的」

6 □ thus「したがって」 □ operation「作戦」 □ create「を作り出す」
□ favorable「良好な，好都合な」 □ condition「条件」 □ development「発達」
□ occur「起きる」

第4段落

[1]Weather modification projects, whether successful or not, bring a variety of problems which make the prospect of large-scale activity in this field very uncertain. [2]Most of the chemicals used in seeding cause pollution, and the disadvantages of these may exceed the advantages achieved by the seeding process. [3]The release of large amounts of heat energy to reduce fog or clouds, or the generation of extensive electric fields to weaken storms may fall into a similar category. [4]But most problematic of all is our inability to restrict the modification effect to the area for which it was intended. [5]For instance, suppressing a hailstorm over a region of farmland might move the storm activity to a neighboring urban area; the crops would be saved, but in the city, windows would be smashed, motorcars damaged, and people seriously injured. [6]One scarcely dares to imagine the legal consequences of such an event.

[1]気象改変計画は，うまくいっても失敗しても，この分野での大規模な活動の見通しをきわめ

て不確かなものにする様々な問題をもたらすことになる。[2]雲の種まきに使われる化学物質のほとんどが大気汚染の原因となり，これらの不利益は種まきの過程で得られる利益よりも大きいかもしれないのだ。[3]霧とか雲を散らすために大量の熱エネルギーを放出したり，嵐を弱体化するために広範囲に電場を作り出したりすることも同じようなカテゴリーに分類できる。[4]しかし何よりも最も問題なのが，気象改変の影響を意図された地域に制限することができないことである。[5]たとえば，農業地帯への雹（ひょう）を伴う嵐を抑えると，その嵐の活動を隣接する都市部へ移すことになるかもしれない。作物は救われるだろうが，街では窓が粉々に割れ，車が被害を受け，人々は重傷を負うことであろう。[6]そうした出来事の法的な結果をあえて想像しようとはまずしない。

2 used in seeding は the chemicals を修飾する過去分詞句。achieved by the seeding process は the advantages を修飾する過去分詞句。

□ chemical「化学物質」　□ pollution「汚染」　□ disadvantage「不利益」
□ process「過程」

3 2つめの or は The release ... reduce fog or clouds と the generation ... weaken storms の2つの名詞句を結んでいる。

□ large amounts of A「大量のA」　□ fog「霧」　□ generation「発生」
□ extensive「広範囲にわたる」　□ electric field「電場」　□ weaken「を弱める」
□ fall into A「Aに分類される」

4 most problematic of all (C) is (V) our inability ... (S)という語順になっている。for which it was intended は the area を修飾する関係代名詞節。

□ problematic「問題のある」　□ A's inability to *do*「Aが…できないこと」
□ restrict A to B「AをBに制限する」　□ effect「影響，効果」
□ be intended for A「Aに向けて意図されている」

5 but 以下では motorcars と people の後ろに繰り返しを避けるため would be が省略されている。

□ for instance「たとえば」　□ suppress「を抑える」　□ region「地域」
□ farmland「農地」　□ move A to B「AをBに移動させる」　□ neighboring「隣接する」
□ urban「都会の」　□ crop「作物」　□ smash「を粉々にする」　□ motorcar「自動車」
□ be seriously injured「重傷を負う」

6 □ scarcely dare to *do*「あえて…しようとはまずしない」　□ legal「法的な」
□ consequences「結果，成り行き」

第5段落

[1]Nor does it stop there. [2]We know that hurricanes and typhoons are one of the

principal mechanisms that transfer heat energy received from the sun in tropical areas to middle and high latitudes. [3]If that mechanism were interfered with, who knows what sort of chain reaction might follow? [4]What kind of major climatic changes might turn up in different parts of the world during subsequent months?

[1]話はそこで終わらない。[2]ハリケーンや台風は，熱帯地域の太陽から受け取った熱エネルギーを中高緯度地域へ運ぶ主要なメカニズムの１つであることを我々は知っている。[3]そのメカニズムが邪魔されたら，いったいどんな連鎖反応が起こるのか誰がわかるだろう。[4]どのような大規模な気象の変化がその後数ヶ月間，世界の各地で起こることになるであろうか。

2 that transfer 以下は the principal mechanisms を修飾する関係代名詞節。received from the sun in tropical areas は heat energy を修飾する過去分詞句。

□ hurricane「ハリケーン」　□ typhoon「台風」　□ principal「主要な，重要な」

□ mechanism「メカニズム，仕組み」　□ transfer A to B「AをBへと運ぶ，移動させる」

□ receive「を受け取る」　□ tropical「熱帯の」

3 if 節は，what sort of chain reaction might follow に対する仮定法過去の条件節。who knows ...? は修辞疑問文で，no one knows .... と言い換えられる。

□ chain reaction「連鎖反応」　□ follow「後に続く」

4 第３文の条件節に対する帰結節になっている。

□ major「大規模な」　□ climatic change「気候変動」　□ turn up「起きる，現れる」

□ subsequent「その後の，次に起こる」

8 名前の持つ魔力

解答

問1　ウ．concealed

問2　昔から，病気がちの子供の名前は，その子供を苦しめている霊がだまされてその子を1人に放っておいてくれるように，変えられている。

問3　イ．responsibility

問4　Bill または bill

問5　何かをヘビと呼ぶと，その物がヘビのように振る舞って人を噛むことがある，と信じられているから。(46字)

問6　イ

設問解説

問1　空所(1)を含む文は，第1段落第1・2文の「人の名前には魔力が備わっている」という内容の具体例を述べている。直後の to prevent 以下に「その名を使うことを通じてその子が魔力に影響されるのを防ぐため」と述べられていることから，「子供の名前は隠されている」と考えるのが最も自然。したがって，正解はウ。

ア.「採用される」イ.「呼ばれる」ウ.「隠される」エ.「暴露される」

問2　so that S will *do* で「S が…するために，…するように」という目的を表す構文。so that 節の中では the spirits が主語で，tormenting it は the spirits を修飾する現在分詞句。また，be deceived と leave the child alone が and で結ばれている。

□ sickly「病気がちの，病弱な」　□ traditionally「伝統的に，従来から」

□ spirit「霊，霊魂」　□ torment「を苦しめる」　□ deceive「をだます」

□ leave O alone「Oを1人にしておく」

問3　空所(3)を含む文の前の文で「しかし，この名前の交換には責任の交換も伴っていた」と述べられていることから，空所には「責任」を表す語を入れるのが最も自然。したがって，正解はイ。

ア.「関連」イ.「責任」ウ.「親しさ」エ.「優越」

問4　最初の空所から，英語圏で人名として使われる名詞であることがわかる。さらに，「電力会社からの(　4　)」「国会を通過する前の(　4　)」および「鳥の

(　4　)」の空所に入れて意味の通る表現を作ることのできる多義語を考える。名詞 bill には「請求書／法案／(鳥の)くちばし」という意味があり，また Bill と大文字で始めれば人名にもなることから，正解は Bill または bill である。

問5 後ろに続く2文がこの文に関する補足説明となっていることを読み取り，その2文めの It is ... bite you. の内容を制限字数に留意してまとめる。

□ acceptable「受け入れ可能な，容認できる」　□ call O C「OをCと呼ぶ」

問6 ア. 第3段落第5文の内容に不一致。「自分の夫や自分の両親の名前」ではなく「自分の夫や夫の両親の名前」を口に出すことが許されていない，と述べられている。

イ. 第4段落第9文の内容に一致。

ウ. 第4段落第7文の内容に不一致。

エ. マルケサス諸島における「初期の探検家の報告」については第2段落第4～7文で述べられているが，「最近の調査」については述べられていない。

Advice 内容説明問題④ 原因・理由の説明

下線部の原因・理由を説明させる問題では，まず下線部の意味を取ったうえで，関連する内容が述べられている箇所を下線部の前後から探すことになる。because や the reason is that ... といった原因・理由を表す表現がある場合は，対応箇所を見つけやすいが，そうでない場合には，「…だから，下線部の内容」という因果関係が成立するかどうかを常に確認しながら，探していくことが大切。本問の問5では，下線部に続く2文に関連する内容が述べられているが，この中で下線部と因果関係が成立するのは2文めの内容である。

要　約

言葉，特に人や物の名前には魔力がある，と信じられている証拠が世界のいたる所にある。魔力の影響を考慮して，特定の言葉を避けたり，他の言葉で代用したりすることもある。

(81字)

▶▶▶ 構文・語句解説 ◀◀◀

第1段落

[1]There is a large amount of evidence which shows that people believe words to have magic powers. [2]This is most easily illustrated with those very special words, people's names. [3]In the traditions of modern Ethiopia, the real name of a child is concealed to prevent the child from being influenced magically through the use of the name. [4]It is believed that knowledge of the name gives power over the person who bears that name.

[1]人々が言葉に魔力が備わっていると信じていることを示す証拠がたくさんある。[2]とても特別な言葉である，人の名前を使って，ごく簡単にこのことは例証できる。[3]現代のエチオピアの伝統では，子供の本名は，その名前を使うことによってその子が魔力に影響されるのを防ぐために秘密にされている。[4]名前を知ることがその名前を持っている人に力を及ぼすと信じられているのである。

1 □ a large amount of A「たくさんのA，大量のA」　□ evidence「証拠」
□ magic power「魔力」
□ believe O to *do*「Oが…すると信じる」*do* の位置には be や have がくる。
2 those very special words と people's names は同格の関係。
□ be illustrated with A「Aを使って例証される」
3 □ tradition「伝統」　□ modern「現代の／近代の」
□ prevent O from *doing*「Oが…するのを防ぐ」　□ influence「に影響を及ぼす」
□ magically「(魔法にかかったかのように)不思議に」
4 □ give power over A「Aに力を及ぼす」　□ bear「を持っている」

第2段落

[1]Beliefs of this type are widespread throughout the world. [2]In Borneo, for example, the name of a sickly child is traditionally changed so that the spirits tormenting it will be deceived and leave the child alone. [3]The spirits, apparently, can recognize people only by their names, not through other characteristics. [4]An extreme example was reported by the early explorers in the Marquesas Islands. [5]There it was possible for two people to exchange names as a sign of mutual respect. [6]But this exchange of names also involved an exchange of responsibilities: obligations concerning the family, friends, and even enemies went with the change of name. [7]A man might even be expected to go to war because of the responsibility to his new name.

[1]この種の考え方は世界中に広がっている。[2]たとえばボルネオでは昔から，病気がちの子供の名前は，その子供を苦しめている霊がだまされてその子を1人に放っておいてくれるように，変えられている。[3]どうも霊は，他の特徴によってではなく，人を名前でしか見分けられないようである。[4]極端な例が，昔マルケサス諸島を探検した人たちによって報告された。[5]そこでは，2人の人がお互いを尊敬する証として名前を交換することが可能であった。[6]しかし，この名前の交換には責任の交換も伴っていた。家族，友人に関する義務，そして敵に関する義務

さえも，名前の変化に伴って移ったのである。7男性の場合，新しい名前に対する責任のために戦争に行かなければならないことさえあった。

1 □ belief「信念，信仰」　□ widespread「広く行き渡った」
□ throughout A「Aのいたるところに，Aじゅうに」
3 only by their names, not through other characteristics は X, not Y「YではなくX」の表現。
□ apparently「〈文修飾で〉どうも…のようだ」
□ recognize「〈人〉が誰だかわかる，の見分けがつく」　□ characteristic「特徴」
4 □ extreme「極端な」　□ report「を報告する」　□ early「初期の」
□ explorer「探検家」
5 □ exchange「を交換する／交換」　□ as a sign of A「A の証として」
□ mutual「相互の，互いの」
6 □ involve「を(必然的に)伴う，含む」　□ obligation「義務，責任」
□ concerning A「Aに関して」　□ go with A「Aとともに移る」
7 □ be expected to *do*「…することになっている」　□ because of A「Aのせいで，Aが原因で」

第3段落

[1]In some cultures, the use of a particular name is an offence. [2]In imperial China, for instance, it was a crime to use the name of a reigning emperor. [3]This could provide problems when the emperor's name was also a common word. [4]If this occurred in an English-speaking country today where the emperor's name was Bill, it would be illegal to talk about a bill from the electricity company, a bill before parliament, or the bill of a bird. [5]Similar prohibitions are found among the Zulus: there a woman is not allowed to utter the name of her husband or the names of his parents.

1文化によっては，ある特定の名前を使うことが罪になる。2たとえば王朝時代の中国では，そのときに君臨している皇帝の名前を使うことは犯罪であった。3皇帝の名前がありふれた単語でもあった場合には，様々な問題を引き起こすこともあった。4もしこのことが王の名前が Bill であるような英語圏の国で起きるなら，電力会社からの bill(請求書)，国会を通過する前の bill(法案)，または鳥の bill(くちばし)について話をすることが違法になるだろう。5同様の禁止事項がズールー族の間で見られる。そこでは女性が夫の名前や夫の両親の名前を口に出すことは許されていないのである。

1 □ particular「特定の」　□ offence「罪，違反」

2 □ imperial「皇帝の／王政の」　□ crime「犯罪」　□ reigning「君臨している」

□ emperor「皇帝」

3 □ provide「を提供する，与える」

4 仮定法過去の文であり，if 節内において，where 以下は an English-speaking country を修飾する関係副詞節。

□ illegal「違法の，非合法的な」　□ electricity company「電力会社」

□ parliament「〈イギリスなどの〉国会」

5 □ similar「よく似た，同様の」　□ prohibition「禁止事項」

□ allow O to *do*「Oが…するのを許す」　□ utter「を口に出す，発話する」

第4段落

[1]Similar kinds of constraints can apply to the names of things, as well as to the names of people. [2]It is fairly common to find a taboo against the use of the name of a powerful animal such as a bear, tiger, or crocodile. [3]Instead, phrases like 'honey-eater' or nicknames like 'Bruin' are used. [4]In parts of Africa and India it is not acceptable to call a snake a 'snake.' [5]Instead, you say things like 'There is a strap' or 'There is a rope.' [6]It is believed that if you call something a snake, it is likely to act like a snake and bite you. [7]In a similar way, Bavarian farmers in Germany traditionally do not call a fox a 'fox,' in case using the word brings the fox and causes it to attack their hens. [8]In a very similar way, we still say 'Talk of the devil,' suggesting that speaking of someone causes them to appear. [9]Finally, and more subtly, it used to be the case in China that a doctor who did not have the appropriate drug for his patient would write the name of the drug on a piece of paper, burn it, and get the patient to eat the ashes. [10]It was believed that the name of the drug would be just as effective as the drug itself.

[1]同種の制約は，人の名前だけでなく事物の名前にも当てはまる。[2]クマやトラやワニのような力の強い動物の名前を使うことに対するタブーが見つかることはとてもよくある。[3]代わりに，「蜂蜜食い」のような表現や「ブルーイン」のようなニックネームが使われる。[4]アフリカやインドの地方では，ヘビを「ヘビ」と呼ぶことが受け入れられていない。[5]その代わりに，「ひもがある」とか「ロープがある」というようなことを言う。[6]何かをヘビと呼ぶと，それがヘビのように振る舞って嚙みつくだろう，と信じられているのだ。[7]同様に，ドイツのバイエルン地方の農夫たちは昔からキツネを「キツネ」と呼ばないが，それはその言葉を使うとキツネを呼び寄せ，自分たちのめんどりを襲う原因となるといけないからである。[8]また同様に，私たちは今でも「うわさをすれば影」と言って，誰かのことを話すとその人が姿を現すことをほの

めかす。[9]最後に，そしてより理解しがたいことだが，患者のための適切な薬がない医者はその薬の名前を紙に書いて燃やし，その灰を患者に食べさせた，というのが中国の実情であった。[10]薬の名前は薬そのものと同じくらい効果がある，と信じられていたのである。

1 □ constraint「制約」　□ apply to A「Aに当てはまる」

□ X as well as Y「XもYも／YだけでなくXも」

2 □ fairly「かなり」　□ taboo against A「Aに関するタブー，禁忌」

□ crocodile「ワニ，クロコダイル」

3 □ instead「その代わりに，そうではなくて」　□ phrase「表現，文句」

□ honey-eater「蜂蜜食い」

□ Bruin「ブルーイン」中世の動物叙事詩 Reynard the Fox に登場するクマの名前から，一般にクマの愛称として使われるようになった。

5 □ strap「ひも」

6 □ be likely to *do*「たぶん…するだろう，…する可能性が高い」

7 in case 節内は using the word が主語であり，brings the fox と causes it to attack their hens の2つの動詞句が and で結ばれている。

□ in a similar way「同様に」　□ in case S V ...「…するといけないから」

□ cause O to *do*「Oに…させる」　□ hen「めんどり」

8 suggesting 以下は分詞構文。

Talk of the devil は「うわさをすれば影」という意味のことわざ。Talk [Speak] of the devil and he will appear. が正式な言い方で，「悪魔のうわさをしてごらん，そうすれば悪魔が姿を現すだろう」という意味。たいていは Talk [Speak] of the devil. の部分だけが使われる。

□ suggest that 節「…ということを示唆する」

9 it used to be the case in China that ... において，it は形式主語で，真主語は that 以下。なお，write the ... of paper と burn it と get the ... the ashes の3つの動詞句が and で結ばれている。

□ subtly「理解しがたいことだが」　□ be the case「実情である」

□ appropriate「適切な」　□ drug「薬」　□ patient「患者」　□ burn「を燃やす」

□ get O to *do*「Oに…させる，してもらう」　□ ash「灰」

10 □ just as ... as ～「～とちょうど同じだけ…」　□ effective「効き目がある，効果的な」

AIの影響

解　答

問 1　しかし，人工知能(AI)を備えたロボットが私たちの生活をどのように変えるのかについての話が取り組んでいないのは，AI のより広範で，ことによるとより意義深い「社会的な」影響，つまり AI が私たち人間のお互いの関わり方にどのように影響しうるのかということである。

問 2　不器用で，ミスを認めて謝るロボットのいる集団の方が，基本的なことしか言わないロボットのいる対照群より，意思疎通がよくなり，より協力できるようになった。(75字)

問 3　AI のせいで，協力する人間の能力が低下しかねないこと。(27字)

問 4　ウ．unselfishly

問 5　ウ．stopped

設問解説

問 1　these stories は直前の文の robots equipped with artificial intelligence (AI) might transform our lives の内容を指している。and は broader と potentially more significant を結んでおり，address の目的語である *social* effects を修飾している。ダッシュ(—)以下は直前の AI's broader and potentially more significant *social* effects を具体的に言い換えたもの。なお，could は「(ひょっとしたら)…することもありえる」という意味。

□ address「に取り組む」　□ broad「広範囲に及ぶ」　□ potentially「ひょっとすると」
□ significant「意義深い」　□ social「社会的な」　□ effect「影響」
□ the way S V ...「…する方法」　□ affect「に影響を与える」　□ humans「人間」
□ interact with A「A と互いに関わる，影響し合う」　□ one another「お互い」

問 2　下線部(2)の「実験の方法」については第２段落第２～５文に述べられ，「実験の結果」については第２段落第６～８文に述べられているので，この内容を制限字数に留意してまとめればよい。

□ study「研究」

問 3　下線部(3)を含む第４段落に「実験の内容とその結果」が述べられている。次の第５段落第１文には「この発見の意味合いを考えてみよう」と述べられ，同段落最終文に The fact that ... extremely concerning. とあるので，この文の

that 節の内容を答えればよい。

□ experiment「実験」

問 4 下線部(4)の直後の第 4 段落第 5 文の「ある回で周りの人に気前よく振る舞うと，次の回で周りの人が自分に気前よく振る舞ってくれ，互恵主義の規範が確立すると，彼らはわかっていたのだ」という内容から，「利他的に行動をした」ことがわかる。したがって，正解はウ。なお，altruistically は難単語であるが，他の選択肢が明らかに不適切であることから解答を引き出す。

ア.「経済的に」 イ.「貪欲に」 ウ.「利他的に」 エ.「利己的に」

問 5 直前の第 4 段落第 7 文に「集団を同様の振る舞いに駆り立てる」と述べられているが，「同様の振る舞い」とは第 6 文に述べられている「自分のお金はそのままにして，周りの人からお金を受け取ること」である。つまり，「集団は利己的に振る舞い，協力することをやめたこと」がわかる。したがって，正解はウ。なお，イは後ろに *doing* ではなく refuse to *do* と to 不定詞が続くので不可。

ア.「…を好んだ」 イ.「…を拒んだ」 ウ.「…をやめた」 エ.「…を欲した」

Advice 語い問題

単語や語句の意味を問う問題では，多義語が狙われる他に，難単語の意味を文脈から推測することが求められることが多い。本問の問 4 では altruistically の意味を知っているかどうかが問われているわけではない。この種の問題では，易しい語句で言い換えられていることが多いので，文脈をしっかりとたどって，その意味を推測することがポイントになる。また，選択肢に与えられた語句で置き換えることで答えが得られることもある。

要 約

人工知能(AI)搭載のロボットは今後，我々人間のお互いの関わり方に良くも悪くも影響を与えることが考えられるが，AI によって協力する人間の能力が低下するとすれば，きわめて危惧すべきことである。(95字)

▶▶▶ 構文・語句解説 ◀◀◀

第 1 段落

[1]Fears about how robots equipped with artificial intelligence (AI) might transform our lives have been a classic part of science fiction for decades. [2]But these stories do not address AI's broader and potentially more significant *social* effects—the ways AI could affect how we humans interact with one another. [3]Putting AI at the center of our lives may change how loving or friendly or kind we are—not just in our direct interactions

with these machines, but in our interactions with one another.

[1]人工知能(AI)を備えたロボットが私たちの生活をどのように変えるのかに関わる不安は，数十年前から SF の典型的な一部であった。[2]しかし，こうした物語が取り組んでいないのは，AI のより広範で，ことによるとより意義深い「社会的な」影響，つまり AI が私たち人間のお互いの関わり方にどのように影響しうるのかということである。[3]AI を生活の中心に置くことで，これらの機械との直接的な関わり方だけでなく私たちの互いへの関わり方において，私たちがどのくらい好意的であったり，友好的であったり，親切であったりするのかを変えてしまうかもしれない。

1 equipped with artificial intelligence (AI) は robots を修飾する過去分詞句。

- ☐ fear「不安」 ☐ equip A with B「AにBを備え付ける」
- ☐ artificial intelligence「人工知能」 ☐ transform「を変える」
- ☐ classic「典型的な／古典の」 ☐ science fiction「SF，空想科学小説」
- ☐ decade「10年間」

3 Putting AI at the center of our lives は主語となる動名詞句。

- ☐ put A at the center of B「AをBの中心に置く」 ☐ loving「好意的な，愛情に満ちた」
- ☐ friendly「友好的な」 ☐ not just X but Y「XだけではなくYもまた」
- ☐ direct「直接の」 ☐ interaction with A「Aとの相互作用」

第2段落

[1]Consider some experiments from my lab at Yale, where my colleagues and I have been exploring how such effects might play out. [2]In one study, we directed small groups of people to work with humanoid robots to lay railroad tracks in a virtual world. [3]Each group consisted of three people and a small blue-and-white robot sitting around a square table, working on tablets. [4]The robot was programmed to make occasional errors and to apologize for them: "Sorry, guys, I made a mistake this round," it declared cheerfully. [5]"I know it may be hard to believe, but robots make mistakes, too." [6]As it turned out, this clumsy confessional robot helped the groups perform *better*—by improving communication among the humans. [7]They became more relaxed and conversational, comforting group members who made a mistake, and laughing together more often. [8]Compared with the control groups, whose robots made only basic statements, the groups with a confessional robot were better able to collaborate.

[1]イェール大学の私の研究室の実験を考えてみよう。そこで同僚と私はそうした影響がどのような結果をもたらすのかを探ってきた。[2]ある研究では，私たちは少人数の人間の集団に，人間に似たロボットと一緒に作業をして仮想空間で鉄道の線路を敷設するよう指示した。[3]それぞれの集団は人間３人と青と白の小型ロボット１台からなり，四角いテーブルを囲んで座り，タブレットで作業した。[4]ロボットはときおりへまをして，それを謝るようプログラムされていた。「すみません，皆さん，今回へまをしてしまいました」と明るく告白したのだった。[5]「信じ難いかもしれませんが，ロボットだってしくじるんですよ」[6]結局，この不器用で告白好きのロボットは集団がよりよく作業するのに役立った。人間同士の意思疎通を改善したのである。[7]３人はより打ち解け，言葉を交わし，しくじった仲間を慰め笑い合うことが増えた。[8]ロボットが基本的な発言しかしなかった対照群と比較すると，告白好きなロボットのいる集団の方がうまく協力できたのだ。

1 where 以下は my lab at Yale を補足説明する非制限用法の関係副詞節。

□ consider「をよく考える」　□ lab「実験室」（＝laboratory）

□ Yale「イェール大学」米国の名門私立大学。　□ colleague「同僚」

□ explore「を研究する，探る」　□ play out「<事が>進展する／<物>が起こる」

2 □ direct O to *do*「Oに…するよう指図する」　□ humanoid「人間の形をした」

□ lay railroad tracks「鉄道の線路を敷設する」　□ virtual world「仮想空間」

3 and は three people と a small blue-and-white robot を結び，sitting 以下は and で結ばれた名詞句を修飾する現在分詞句。working on tablets は sitting around a square table を修飾する分詞構文。

□ consist of A「Aから成り立つ」　□ square「四角い」

□ work on a tablet「タブレットで作業する」

4 and は to make occasional errors と to apologize for them を結んでいる。

□ be programmed to *do*「…するようプログラムされている」　□ occasional「ときおりの」

□ error「間違い」　□ apologize for A「Aのことで謝る」　□ guys「（呼びかけで）君たち」

□ round「（競技の１部となる）１試合，１勝負」　□ declare「を明言する／を宣言する」

□ cheerfully「陽気に」

5 but は I know ... to believe と robots make mistakes, too の２つの節を結んでいる。

6 □ as it turned out「結局は，後でわかったことだが」　□ clumsy「不器用な」

□ confessional「告白する」　□ help O *do*「Oが…するのに役立つ」

□ perform well「うまくいく，調子よく機能する」　□ by *doing*「…することによって」

□ improve「を改善する」　□ communication「意思疎通，コミュニケーション」

7 １つめの and は relaxed と conversational を結び，２つめの and は comforting group members

who made a mistake と laughing together more often の分詞構文を結んでいる。

□ relaxed「くつろいで」　□ conversational「話好きな」　□ comfort「を慰める」

8 whose robots made only basic statements は the control groups を補足説明する非制限用法の関係代名詞節。with a confessional robot は the groups を修飾する形容詞句。

□ compared with A「Aと比較すると」　□ basic「基本的な」　□ statement「発言」

□ collaborate「協力する」

第3段落

[1]This study demonstrates that in systems where people and robots interact socially, the right kind of AI can improve the way humans relate to one another. [2]But adding AI to our social environment can also make us behave less productively and less ethically.

[1]この研究は人間とロボットが親しく関わる組織では，適切な類の AI は人間同士の付き合い方を改善することがあるということを示している。[2]しかし，私たちの社会環境に AI を加えることで，行動の生産性や倫理性が下がることもまたありうる。

1 where people and robots interact socially は systems を修飾する関係副詞節。

□ demonstrate that 節「…ということを明らかにする」　□ interact「互いに関わる」

□ socially「社会的に／親しく」　□ a kind of A「ある種類のA」

□ relate to A「Aとうまく付き合う／Aと関係する」

2 and は less productively と less ethically を結んでいる。

□ add A to B「AをBに加える，付け足す」　□ social「社会的な」

□ environment「環境」　□ make O *do*「Oに…させる」

□ behave「行動する，振る舞う」　□ productively「生産的に」　□ ethically「倫理的に」

第4段落

[1]In another experiment designed to explore how AI might affect the “tragedy of the commons”—the notion that individuals’ self-centered actions may collectively damage their common interests—we gave several thousand subjects money to use over multiple rounds of an online game. [2]In each round, subjects were told that they could either keep their money or donate some or all of it to their neighbors. [3]If they made a donation, we would also make a donation, doubling the money their neighbors received. [4]Early in the game, two-thirds of players acted altruistically. [5]They realized that being generous to their neighbors in one round might prompt their neighbors to be generous to them in the next

one, establishing a norm of reciprocity. [6]From a selfish and short-term point of view, however, the best outcome would be to keep your own money and receive money from your neighbors. [7]In this experiment, we found that by adding just a few bots (posing as human players) that behaved in a selfish way, we could drive the group to behave similarly. [8]Eventually, the human players stopped cooperating altogether. [9]The bots thus converted a group of generous people into selfish ones.

[1]AI が「共有地の悲劇」—個人の自己中心的な行動が全体として共通の利益を損ないかねないという考え—にどのように影響を及ぼすのかを探るよう意図された別の実験で，私たちは数千人の被験者に数回にわたるオンラインゲームで使えるお金を与えた。[2]それぞれの回で，被験者はお金を取っておいてもいいし，周りの人に一部または全部を寄付してもいいと言われた。[3]もし被験者が寄付をすれば，私たちも寄付をするので，周りの人が受け取るお金は倍になる。[4]ゲームの序盤では，参加者の 3 分の 2 が利他的な行動をした。[5]ある回で周りの人に気前よく振る舞うと，次の回で周りの人が自分に気前よく振る舞ってくれ，互恵主義の規範が確立すると，彼らはわかっていたのだ。[6]しかし，利己的で短期的な視点からすると，最善の結果は自分のお金はそのままにして，周りの人からお金を受け取ることであった。[7]この実験で，私たちは（人間の参加者のふりをしている）利己的に振る舞うほんの数台のボットを加えることで，集団を同様の振る舞いに駆り立てることができるとわかった。[8]結局，人間の参加者は協力するのを完全にやめてしまった。[9]こうしてボットは気前のいい人々の集団を利己的な集団に変換したのだ。

1 designed to ... the commons” は another experiment を修飾する過去分詞句。ダッシュ以下は the “tragedy of the commons” の内容を具体的に言い換えたもの。that individuals’ ... common interests は the notion と同格となる名詞節。

□ (be) designed to *do*「…するよう意図されている」　□ tragedy「悲劇」
□ the commons「共有地，公有地」　□ notion「考え」　□ individual「個人」
□ self-centered「自己中心的な」　□ action「行動」　□ collectively「全体的に」
□ common「共通の」　□ interest「利益」　□ subject「被験者」　□ over A「Aの間中」
□ multiple「複数の」　□ online「オンラインの」

2 1つめの or は keep their money と donate some or all of it to their neighbors を結び，2つめの or は some と all を結んでいる。

□ tell O that 節「Oに…と言う」　□ either X or Y「XかYかどちらか」
□ donate A to B「AをBに寄付する，与える」　□ neighbor「隣人，近所の人」

3 仮定法過去の文。doubling 以下は分詞構文。their neighbors received は the money を修飾する

関係代名詞節。

☐ donation「寄付」　☐ double「を２倍にする」　☐ receive「を受け取る」

5 establishing 以下は分詞構文。

☐ realize that 節「…だとわかる」　☐ generous「気前のよい」

☐ prompt O to *do*「Oに…するよう促す」　☐ establish「を確立する」　☐ norm「規範」

6 １つめの and は selfish と short-term を結び，２つめの and は keep your own money と receive money from your neighbors を結んでいる。

☐ selfish「利己的な」　☐ short-term「短期的な」　☐ point of view「見方，観点」

☐ however「しかし」　☐ outcome「結果」

7 posing as human players は a few bots を修飾する現在分詞句。that behaved in a selfish way は a few bots を修飾する関係代名詞節。

☐ pose as A「Aのふりをする」　☐ drive O to *do*「Oに…するように駆り立てる」

8 ☐ eventually「結局」　☐ cooperate「協力する」　☐ altogether「完全に，すっかり」

9 ☐ thus「こうして」　☐ convert A into B「AをBに変える」　☐ one「人」

第５段落

[1]Let's pause to think about the implications of this finding. [2]Cooperation is a key feature of our species, essential for social life. [3]And trust and generosity are crucial in differentiating successful groups from unsuccessful ones. [4]If everyone contributes and makes sacrifices in order to help the group, everyone should benefit. [5]When this behavior breaks down, however, the notion of reciprocity disappears, and everyone suffers. [6]The fact that AI might meaningfully reduce our ability to work together is extremely concerning.

[1]改めてこの発見の意味合いを考えてみよう。[2]協力は私たち人間の重要な特徴であり，社会生活にとっては不可欠である。[3]そして，信頼と気前のよさは，成功する集団と成功しない集団とを分かつのに極めて重要である。[4]もし集団を助けるために誰もが寄付をして犠牲を払うなら，誰もが利益を得るはずである。[5]しかし，この行動が崩壊すると，互恵主義の概念が消失し，誰もが損害を被る。[6]AI が私たちの協力し合う能力を著しく下げかねないという事実は，きわめて厄介である。

1 ☐ pause to think「改めて考える」　☐ implication「意味合い」　☐ finding「発見」

2 essential for social life は a key feature of our species を言い換えたもの。

☐ cooperation「協力」　☐ key「主要な」　☐ feature「特徴」　☐ species「(生物の)種」

□ essential「必要不可欠な」

3 文頭の And は直前の第2文とこの第3文を結んでいる。2つめの and は trust と generosity を結んでいる。ones は groups の代用。

□ trust「信頼」　□ generosity「気前のよさ」　□ crucial「極めて重要な」

□ differentiate A from B「AをBと区別する」　□ successful「成功した」

□ unsuccessful「失敗した」

4 and は contributes と makes sacrifices を結んでいる。

□ contribute「寄付をする」　□ make a sacrifice「犠牲を払う」

□ in order to *do*「…するために」　□ benefit「恩恵を受ける」

5 and は the notion of reciprocity disappears と everyone suffers の2つの節を結んでいる。

□ behavior「行動」　□ break down「故障する／失敗する」

□ disappear「消える，なくなる」　□ suffer「損害を受ける／苦しむ」

6 that AI ... work together は The fact の内容を述べる同格の名詞節。

□ meaningfully「意味ありげに，意味深長に」　□ reduce「を減らす」

□ extremely「極度に，非常に」　□ concerning「厄介な，心配をかける」

10 赤ちゃんを左側に抱く理由

解　答

問1　母親の赤ちゃんに対する振舞い方の１つか２つの側面を考察することは価値がある。

問2　ウ

問3　エ．True

問4　22

問5　the fact that the heart is on the left side of

問6　これは奇妙に聞こえるかもしれないが，それにもかかわらずこれが正しい説明であることを明らかにする調査がいくつか今までに行われている。

問7　ア．crying

設問解説

問1　it is worth *doing* は「…することは価値がある」という意味の表現。また，the way S V ... は「…する方法，様子」という意味。ここでは「母親が赤ちゃんに対して振舞う方法」が直訳。

□ look at A「Aを考察する，観察する」　□ aspect「側面」

問2　下線部(2)は，holding 以下が分詞構文で，「母親の80パーセントが，左腕で乳児を抱いてあやし，身体の左側にかかえていること」という意味。その理由として第１段落第４・５文で「母親は利き腕である右手を使えるように赤ちゃんを左側に抱く」という説が述べられているが，第６文でこれを否定している。第２段落で「赤ちゃんが胎内で聞き慣れた鼓動音が聞こえるように心臓のある左側に抱く」という説が述べられ，これを裏づける調査が第３段落にある。したがって，正解はウ。

□ cradle「をあやす，そっと抱く」　□ infant「乳児」

問3　空所(3)の直前には「左腕で赤ちゃんを抱くことで，母親は利き腕を使えるように空けておくということは実情ではない」とあり，「母親は利き腕である右手を使えるように赤ちゃんを左側に抱く」という説を否定している。空所(3)の後ろでは「右利きと左利きの女性の間では違いはある」といったん否定した説を裏づけることを述べた上で，but 以下には「利き腕に関係なく大多数の母親が赤ちゃんを左側に抱く」という内容が続き，「母親は利き腕である右手を使えるように赤ちゃんを左側に抱く」という説を再度否定している。True, S V ..., but ～「確かに…であるが，～」は前に述べた内容と反対の内容を but の前で譲歩的に述べた上で，but 以下で前の内容に戻ることで強調するという文脈で用いられる。したがって，エが正解。

例 He's done nothing. True, he is clever, but he's not very helpful.
「彼は何もしていない。確かに頭はいいが，あまり役に立たない」

ア.「たとえば」 イ.「そのうえ」 ウ.「したがって」 エ.「確かに」

問4 空所(4)を含む文の文頭にある In other words「言い換えれば」は，その前に述べた内容と同じことを，別の言葉で言い換えるときに用いられる。前の文の but 以下は so＋助動詞＋S「Sもまたそうである」の表現で，ここでは「左利きの母親の78パーセントも左側に赤ちゃんを抱く」という意味。したがって，「左利きの母親の中で利き手を何かをやるために空けておく」，つまり「右手で赤ちゃんを抱く」母親の割合は22パーセントになる。

問5 下線部(5)を含む文の主語 The only other clue とは第1段落で述べられた「母親は利き腕である右手を使えるように赤ちゃんを左側に抱く」こと以外の手がかりのことである。第2段落第4文以降で，「赤ちゃんが胎内で聞き慣れた鼓動音を聞けるように心臓のある左側に抱く」という説が紹介されている。したがって，「他に唯一考えられる手がかりは，心臓が母親の身体の左側にあるという事実から得られる」という意味になるように the fact that the heart is on the left side of と並べ換えればよい。that 以下は the fact と同格の名詞節である。

問6 but 以下の文の構造の把握がポイント。carry A out「Aを行う」が受動態で用いられ，which 以下は tests を修飾する関係代名詞節。このように，関係代名詞節と修飾される名詞が離れていることがある。なお，it は this を指している。

例 Only those people were invited to the party who were interesting to talk to.
「話をして面白い人だけがそのパーティーに招待された」

□ sound C「Cに聞こえる」 □ reveal that 節「…を明らかにする」
□ nevertheless「それにもかかわらず，やはり」 □ explanation「説明」

問7 「鼓動音を聞かされなかったグループは，何をやった結果，ずっと多くのエネルギーを消費していたのか」を考える。第3段落第3文に「鼓動音が流されていない時間の60パーセントの間泣いていたが，この数字が，鼓動音が流されているときにはわずか38パーセントに下がった」とあるので，正解はア。

ア.「泣くこと」 イ.「食べること」 ウ.「眠ること」 エ.「聞くこと」

Advice ディスコース・マーカー①

文と文との意味の関係，論旨の展開をはっきりさせるために用いられる表現があり，ディスコース・マーカーと呼ばれる。本問の問3で問われている True, S V ..., but ～ もそうした表現の1つである。空所補充問題で問われる以外に，こうした表現が解答のヒントになることも多い。またディスコース・マーカーに着目することが論旨の展開を把握するのにも役立つ。

1．追加・列挙

順序立てて何かを列挙するとき，前に述べたことにさらに情報を追加するときに用いる。

「第1に」first(ly) / first of all / in the first place / to begin with

「次に」second(ly) / next / then

「そのうえ」furthermore / moreover / what is more / in addition / besides

「最後に」finally / last(ly) / last of all

2．例示・明確化

前に述べた内容に具体例を挙げるときや，同じ内容を別の言葉で言い換えるときに用いる。

「たとえば」for example / for instance / such as

「言い換えれば」in other words / to put it another way / that is (to say)

本問の問4では，in other words が解答する際のヒントになっている。

要 約

大多数の母親が赤ちゃんを左側に抱くのは，利き腕である右手を使えるようにするためではなく，赤ちゃんが胎内で聞き慣れた鼓動音が聞こえるように心臓のある左側に抱くからである。(84字)

▶▶▶ 構文・語句解説 ◀◀◀

第1段落

[1]It is worth looking at one or two aspects of the way a mother behaves towards her baby. [2]The usual fondling, cuddling and cleaning require little comment, but the position in which she holds the baby against her body when resting is rather revealing. [3]Careful American studies have disclosed that 80 per cent of mothers cradle their infants in their left arms, holding them against the left side of their bodies. [4]If asked to explain the significance of this preference, most people reply that it is obviously due to the fact that

more mothers are right-handed. [5]By holding the babies in their left arms, the mothers keep their dominant arm free for manipulations. [6]But a detailed analysis shows that this is not the case. [7]True, there is a slight difference between right-handed and left-handed females, but not enough to provide an adequate explanation. [8]It emerges that 83 per cent of right-handed mothers hold the baby on the left side, but then so do 78 per cent of left-handed mothers. [9]In other words, only 22 per cent of the left-handed mothers have their dominant hands free for actions. [10]Clearly there must be another less obvious explanation.

[1]母親の赤ちゃんに対する振舞い方の1つか2つの側面を考察することは価値がある。[2]いつものように撫でてやることや抱きしめてやること，清潔にしてやることは特に説明する必要はないが，母親が赤ちゃんを眠っているときに抱く身体に対する位置から明らかになることがかなりある。[3]慎重に行われたアメリカでの研究によって，母親の80パーセントが，左腕で乳児を抱いてあやし，身体の左側にかかえていることがわかった。[4]このような優先傾向の意味を説明するように求められると，それは明らかに右利きの母親の方が多いという事実によるものである，とたいていの人は答える。[5]左腕で赤ちゃんを抱くことで，母親は利き腕を使えるように空けておくのである。[6]しかし，詳しく分析すると，これが実情ではないことがわかる。[7]確かに，右利きと左利きの女性の間ではわずかな違いはあるものの，十分な説明になるほどの違いではない。[8]右利きの母親の83パーセントが左側に赤ちゃんを抱く一方で，左利きの母親の78パーセントも同じようにすることが明らかになる。[9]言い換えれば，左利きの母親の中で利き手を何かをするために空けておく者は22パーセントしかいないのである。[10]明らかに，すぐにはわからないような説明が他にあるに違いない。

2 when resting = when it is resting

□ require「を必要とする」　□ rest「眠る，休む」

□ revealing「〈隠された事実などを〉明らかにする」

3 □ disclose「を明らかにする」

4 If asked to explain ... = If they are asked to explain ...

that more mothers are right-handed は the fact と同格の名詞節。

□ significance「意味」　□ preference「優先傾向，より好むこと」　□ obviously「明らかに」

□ S be due to A「SはAのせいである」　□ right-handed「右利きの」

5 □ keep O C「OをCにしておく」　□ manipulation「操作」

6 □ detailed「詳しい」　□ analysis「分析」　□ be the case「実情である」

7 but not enough to provide ... = but there is not enough difference to provide ...

□ slight「わずかな」　□ left-handed「左利きの」　□ female「女性」

□ adequate「十分な，適切な」

8 □ emerge「明らかになる，現れる」　□ but then「しかし一方では」

9 □ have O C「OをCにする」

10 □ obvious「見てすぐわかる，明白な」

第2段落

[1]The only other clue comes from the fact that the heart is on the left side of the mother's body. [2]Could it be that the sound of her heart-beat is the vital factor? [3]And in what way? [4]Thinking along these lines it was argued that perhaps during its existence inside the body of the mother, the growing embryo becomes fixated on the sound of the heart-beat. [5]If this is so, then the re-discovery of this familiar sound after birth might have a calming effect on the infant, especially as it has just been thrust into a strange and frighteningly new world outside. [6]If this is so, then the mother, either instinctively or unconsciously, would soon arrive at the discovery that her baby is more at peace if held on the left against her heart, than on the right.

[1]他に唯一考えられる手がかりは，心臓が母親の身体の左側にあるという事実から得られる。[2]母親の鼓動の音が決定的な要因であるということはありえるだろうか？[3]またどのようにありえるだろう？[4]この方向で考えて，おそらく母親の胎内にいる間に，成長する胎児は鼓動の音を心の奥底に記憶すると論じられた。[5]もしそうであれば，誕生後この聞き慣れた音を再発見することは，特に見知らぬ，恐ろしいほど目新しい外界へ押し出されたばかりの時には，乳児に対して沈静効果を持つかもしれない。[6]そうだとすれば，母親は，本能的にあるいは無意識のうちに，赤ちゃんは右側よりも，心臓にあたる左側に抱くと安心することをすぐに発見することになるだろう。

1 □ clue「手がかり」

2 □ it could be that 節「…ということがありえる」

□ heart-beat「心臓の鼓動」　□ vital「決定的な，極めて重要な」　□ factor「要因」

3 in what way? = in what way could it be that the sound of her heart-beat is the vital factor?

4 □ thinking along these lines「この方向で考えて」　□ argue「と論じる，主張する」

5 If this is so の this は第4文の that 節の内容を指す。

□ re-discovery「再発見」　□ calming「落ち着かせる」　□ effect「効果」

□ thrust A into B「AをBに押し出す」　□ frighteningly「恐ろしいほど」

6 If this is so の this は第5文の内容を指す。that 以下は the discovery と同格の名詞節。

if held on the left ... ＝if it is held on the left ...

□instinctively「本能的に」　□unconsciously「無意識のうちに」　□at peace「安らかな」

第３段落

[1]This may sound strange, but tests have now been carried out which reveal that it is nevertheless the true explanation. [2]Groups of new-born babies in a hospital nursery were exposed for a considerable time to the recorded sound of a heart-beat at a standard rate of 72 beats per minute. [3]There were nine babies in each group and it was found that one or more of them was crying for 60 per cent of the time when the sound was not switched on, but that this figure fell to only 38 per cent when the heart-beat recording was thumping away. [4]The heart-beat groups also showed a greater weight-gain than the others, although the amount of food taken was the same in both cases. [5]Clearly the beatless groups were burning up a lot more energy as a result of the vigorous actions of their crying.

[1]これは奇妙に聞こえるかもしれないが，それにもかかわらずこれが正しい説明であることを明らかにする調査がいくつか今までに行われている。[2]病院の育児室にいる新生児のグループに，１分間に72回という標準的な脈拍の録音された鼓動音を相当期間聞かせた。[3]それぞれのグループには９人の赤ちゃんがいて，そのうちの少なくとも１人以上が，音が流されていない時間の60パーセントの間泣いていたが，この数字が，鼓動の録音がドキンドキンと鳴っているときにはわずか38パーセントに下がることが判明した。[4]鼓動音を聞かされたグループはまた，もう一方のグループと比べて，摂取した食事の量はいずれでも同じであったにもかかわらず，体重の増加が著しかった。[5]明らかに，鼓動音を聞かされなかったグループは，泣くという激しい運動の結果，ずっと多くのエネルギーを消費していたのである。

2 □nursery「育児室」　□expose A to B「AをBにさらす」

□considerable「相当な，かなりの」　□standard「標準的な」

3 □switch A on「Aのスイッチを入れる」　□figure「数字」

4 the amount of food taken の taken は food を修飾する形容詞用法の過去分詞。

□weight-gain「体重の増加」

5 □beatless「鼓動音のない」名詞＋less で「…がない」という意味の形容詞を作る。

□burn A up「A〈エネルギーなど〉を使い尽くす，消費する」

□a lot＋比較級「はるかに…，ずっと…」　□vigorous「激しい，活発な」

11 睡眠

解答

問1　(1a) ウ. conflicting　(1b) イ. physical
問2　イ
問3　1. 語い力の低下　2. 集中力の低下　3. 話し言葉の不明瞭化
問4　Why is it that most of us want more sleep
問5　(5a) イ　(5b) エ
問6　人間は一度ではなく二度眠るように作られたのであり，昼食後に10分昼寝をすると，たいていの人は気分がよくなるものである。

設問解説

問1　(1a)次の2文に「私たちには睡眠を求める気持ちがある反面，睡眠をとりすぎることを不安に思う気持ちもある」と述べられているので，私たちは睡眠に対して「相反する」気持ちを抱いていることがわかる。したがって，正解はウ。
ア.「肯定的な」イ.「否定的な」ウ.「相反する」エ.「思慮深い」
(1b)第2段落で「睡眠不足はハツカネズミに身体的な影響を大いに与える」という内容が述べられているのに対して，空所を含む文の次の文では「一晩よく眠れなかったからといって，体力や調整能力や気力が落ちることはほとんどない」と述べられているので，「人間は睡眠不足から身体的な問題を被ることは少ない」ことがわかる。したがって，正解はイ。なお，on the other hand「ところが一方」という表現もヒントになる。
ア.「精神的な」イ.「身体的な」ウ.「科学的な」エ.「異なった」

問2　下線部(2)の疑問文に続いて，第2～4段落で動物と人間とでは睡眠を必要とする理由が異なっていることが述べられているが，その要点は「人間は動物と違って身体的には睡眠を必要としていない」ことである。そして，第4段落第4文で「私たちの脳は，睡眠が提供してくれる休息を大いに必要としているようである」と述べられているので，正解はイ。

問3　下線部(3)の直後の文に述べられている3つの内容を簡潔にまとめる。
□ function「機能」　□ suffer「悪くなる，質が落ちる」
□ sharply「ひどく，はっきりと」

問4　下線部(4)を含む文の最後に疑問符が打たれていることに注目し，疑問文を構成する。この文で提起した疑問に対する答えが続く2つの段落で提示されていることから，「なぜ私たちは(可能であれば)より多くの睡眠を欲するのだろうか」という意味の疑問文を作ればよいことがわかる。疑問詞＋is it that ...？は疑問詞を強調する強調構文であり，Why is it that ...？は「…はいったいなぜなのか？」という意味。

問5 アメリカ人の研究者の考えは，下線部(5a)を含む文の that 以下に述べられている。ヨーロッパの研究者の考えは，下線部(5b)を含む文の that 以下，および次の文に述べられている。

ア.「私たちは日中10分間の昼寝をするべきである」

イ.「たいていの人は実際に眠っているよりも夜により多くの時間眠る必要がある」

ウ.「私たちは好きなだけ多くの時間眠るべきである」

エ.「私たちが睡眠が好きだからといって，睡眠をとる必要があるということにはならない」

問6 ここでの S is made to *do* は「Sは～するようにできている」の意味。使役動詞 make の受動態と混同しないこと。一方，後半は使役動詞 make O *do* を用いた形。使役動詞 make が無生物主語で用いられると，主語が原因・理由を表し，「SのおかげでOは…する」と訳出する。なお，will は習性を表し「…するものだ」という意味。

例1 Mr. Tanaka is made to be a scientist.
「田中さんは科学者になるように生まれてきたようなものだ」

例2 I was made to go on a business trip to Tokyo yesterday for my boss.
「昨日は上司の代わりに東京に出張させられました」

例3 His joke made me laugh a lot.
「彼の冗談のせいで，大いに笑ってしまった」

□ not X but Y「XではなくY」　□ nap「昼寝，仮眠」

Advice ディスコース・マーカー②

3．逆接・対比

前に述べた内容に反することや，対照的なことを述べるときに用いる。逆接のディスコース・マーカーの後ろで，筆者の主張や論点が述べられていることも多い。また，逆接・対比の意味の関係が成立するように空所を補充させる問題は頻出である。

「しかし」but / (and) yet / however / nevertheless / still

「一方で」on the other hand / by[in] contrast

4．因果関係

原因，結果の関係を明確に述べるときに用いる。

「したがって」so / consequently / therefore / thus / hence / as a result / for this reason / because of this / this is why S＋V ...

「それは…だからだ」after all / this is because S V ... / the reason for this is that S V ...

本問の問1では，yet と on the other hand が解答する際のヒントになっている。

要約

最近の研究によれば，人間は他の動物と違い，身体ではなく脳に休息を与えるために眠るようである。必要とされる睡眠時間に関してはいろいろな議論があるが，昼寝が効果的であることはわかっている。(92字)

構文・語句解説

第1段落

[1]Humans have long conceived conflicting sentiments about sleep. [2]We want it, enjoy it and despair when we can't get enough of it. [3]Yet we also have a fear of getting too much. [4]Napoleon recommended six hours of sleep each night for a man, seven for a woman and eight for a fool.

[1]人間は長い間睡眠に関して相反する気持ちを抱いてきた。[2]睡眠を求め，楽しみ，また睡眠を十分に得られないと絶望する。[3]しかし，睡眠をとりすぎているのではという不安も抱えている。[4]ナポレオンは男性には毎晩6時間，女性には7時間，愚か者には8時間の睡眠を勧めた。

1 □ humans「人間」　□ long「長い間」（＝for a long time）

□ conceive「〈考えなど〉を抱く」　□ sentiment「気持ち」

2 3つの it はいずれも sleep を指す。　□ despair「絶望する」

□ get enough of A「Aを十分に手にする」

4 □ recommend「を勧める」

第2段落

[1]Why do we need sleep, and how much of it should we get? [2]Scientists are beginning to answer the questions, and believe that humans sleep for different reasons than other animals. [3]In experiments, mice have been shown to suffer physically from lack of sleep. [4]After a few days, they begin to lose weight, although they eat a lot. [5]After 14 days, they die.

[1]なぜ私たちは睡眠を必要としているのだろうか，またどれだけの睡眠をとるべきなのだろうか？[2]科学者はこの問題を解明し始めていて，人間は他の動物とは違う理由で眠ると考えるようになっている。[3]実験によると，ハツカネズミは睡眠不足により身体的に苦しむことが証明されている。[4]たくさん食べているのに，数日後には体重が減り始める。[5]14日後には死んでしまうのである。

2 answer the questions と believe 以下が and で結ばれている。
□ different A than B「Bとは違うA」

3 □ experiment「実験」　□ mice＜mouse「ハツカネズミ」の複数形。
□ be shown to *do*「…すると証明される」　□ suffer from A「A〈病気など〉で苦しむ」
□ physically「身体的に」　□ lack「不足，欠如」

第3段落

[1]Humans, on the other hand, usually show few physical problems from lack of sleep. [2]A bad night's sleep will cause little reduction in strength, coordination or stamina. [3]Yet cognitive function suffers sharply. [4]Our vocabulary drops measurably; we are unable to concentrate for long periods; our speech may become unclear.

[1]ところが人間は普通，睡眠不足による身体的な問題を示すことは少ない。[2]一晩よく眠れなかったからといって，体力や調整能力や気力が落ちることはほとんどない。[3]しかし，認識機能はひどく損なわれる。[4]語い力は相当に落ち，長い間集中することができなくなり，話し方がはっきりしなくなることもある。

2 □ cause「を引き起こす」　□ reduction in A「Aの減少」　□ strength「体力」
□ stamina「気力，スタミナ」

4 □ vocabulary「語い力」　□ measurably「かなり，目に見えて」

□ concentrate「集中する」　□ speech「話し方，発話」

第4段落

[1]Why the difference between humans and other animals? [2]Scientists reason that humans have learned to rest their bodies even in a waking state. [3]The difference in metabolic rate between a person lying down and one who is asleep may be as little as 5 percent. [4]Yet our brains, it seems, very much need the rest that sleep provides.

[1]人間と他の動物の間に違いがあるのはなぜだろう？[2]科学者は，人間は目覚めている状態でも身体を休めることができるようになっている，と考えている。[3]横になっている人と眠っている人との間の代謝率の違いはわずか5パーセントかもしれない。[4]しかし，私たちの脳は，睡眠が提供してくれる休息を大いに必要としているようである。

1 Why の後ろに名詞句のみを置くことがある。

□ difference between A and B「AとBの違い」

2 □ reason that 節「…と論じる，推論する」　□ learn to *do*「…できるようになる」

□ rest「を休ませる，に休養を与える」　□ waking「目覚めている」

□ state「状態」

3 □ as little as＋数詞「わずか…，…ほど少ない」

4 our brains, it seems, very much need ... ＝it seems that our brains very much need ...

□ provide「を与える，提供する」

第5段落

[1]The recommended amount of sleep has been disputed in recent years. [2]Humans have strange sleep patterns, usually getting six to eight hours a night during the working week, and up to 10 on weekends. [3]Why is it that most of us want more sleep if we can get it?

[1]近年，推奨される睡眠の量が議論されている。[2]人間は奇妙な睡眠パターンを持っており，平日は一晩に6時間から8時間眠り，週末には10時間も眠るのが普通である。[3]私たちはできればもっと眠りたいと思うのはいったいなぜだろう？

1 □ dispute「を議論する」　□ recent「最近の」

2 usually getting ... on weekends は分詞構文。　□ the working week「平日／週労働時間」

☐ up to A「(最高) Aまで，Aに至るまで」

第6・7段落

[1]American researchers now argue that humans need a minimum of nine hours' sleep each night. [2]These scientists theorize that we are deprived of sleep most of the time. [3]As proof, they cite the drowsiness most of us feel at some point during the day.

[4]European researchers challenge this notion, asserting that there is such a thing as sleep gluttony. [5]The fact that we like sleep does not mean we need it.

[1]アメリカの研究者は今，人間は毎晩最低9時間の睡眠が必要である，と論じている。[2]これらの研究者は，私たちはほとんどいつでも睡眠を奪われている，と推論している。[3]彼らは証拠として，日中のある時点で私たちのほとんどが感じる眠気を挙げる。

[4]ヨーロッパの研究者はこの考えに異議を唱えており，睡眠をむさぼる性質といったものがあると主張している。[5]睡眠が好きだという事実は，睡眠が必要だということを意味してはいない。

1 ☐ researcher「研究者」　☐ argue that 節「…と論じる，主張する」
☐ minimum「最低限」

2 ☐ theorize that 節「…だと推論する，…だと理論上想定する」
☐ deprive A of B「AからBを奪う」　☐ most of the time「たいていは，ほとんどいつも」

3 ☐ cite「を(例として)挙げる，引き合いに出す」　☐ drowsiness「眠気」
☐ at some point「ある時点で」　☐ during the day「日中，昼間に」

4 asserting 以下は連続の結果を表す分詞構文で，「そして…と主張している」という意味。
☐ challenge「に異議を唱える，を疑う」　☐ notion「考え，意見」
☐ assert that 節「…だと主張する」

5 that we like sleep は The fact と同格の名詞節。

第8・9段落

[1]Studies support the European view. [2]If people are given the opportunity to sleep longer, for instance, they may not feel tired until a later hour the next day. [3]The extra hour in bed may do nothing more than adjust our daily rhythm.

[4]Experts say the drowsiness many of us feel during the day may not be because we had too little sleep at night, but because we need an early afternoon nap. [5]Humans were made to sleep not once, but twice, and a 10-minute nap after lunch will make most of us

feel better. [6]This is the reason so many cultures keep the siesta hour.

[1]いろいろな研究がヨーロッパの考えを支持している。[2]たとえば，人々はより長く眠る機会を与えられると，その次の日はより遅い時間まで疲れを感じないかもしれない。[3]ベッドで過ごす余分な時間は，私たちの日々の生活リズムを調整しているだけかもしれない。

[4]専門家によると，私たちの多くが日中感じる眠気は夜の睡眠が少なすぎたからではなく，午後の早いうちに昼寝が必要だからなのである。[5]人間は一度ではなく二度眠るように作られたのであり，昼食後に10分昼寝をすると，たいていの人は気分がよくなるものである。[6]これがとても多くの文化にシエスタの時間が残っている理由である。

1 □ study「研究」

2 □ opportunity to *do*「…する機会」　□ until a later hour「より遅い時間まで」

3 □ extra「余分な」　□ do nothing more than *do*「…するだけだ」

□ adjust「を調整する，調節する」　□ daily rhythm「日々の生活リズム」

4 may not be because ... but because ... は not X but Y「X ではなく Y」の表現を用いたもの。many of us feel during the day は the drowsiness を修飾する関係代名詞節。

□ expert「専門家」

6 so 以下は reason を修飾する関係副詞節。

□ siesta「シエスタ」スペイン，イタリア，ラテンアメリカ諸国に見られる昼寝の習慣のこと。

12 触れることの大切さ

解答

問1　世の中について書くためには，手を伸ばして触れてみる必要があるということ。(36字)

問2　ヘレン・ケラーの像に触れると，見たときには気づかなかった重さ，深さ，形，個性を感じられたということ。(50字)

問3　目だけを使って見るときには，私たちはまさに目の前にあるものだけに限られてしまう。

問4　ア．commonplace

問5　イ．extraordinary development

問6　今日私たちは，どんなものでも完全に理解するのに触れることがいかに重要であるのかに気づいている。

問7　エ．Do touch

▶▶▶ 設問解説 ◀◀◀

問1「このアドバイス」とは第1段落にあるマーク・トウェインの語ったアドバイスのことである。第1文で比喩的に語ったものを具体的に述べたのが第2文なので，第2文をまとめる。なお，2つの it はいずれも the world を指している。

問2 下線部(2)は「その違いは驚くべきものだった」という意味。「その違い」とはヘレン・ケラーの像を見ていたときと，手で触れたときの違いである。また，「驚くべきものだった」については，次の文に具体的に述べられている。

問3 be limited to A「Aに限られている」の A の位置に関係代名詞 what で導かれた名詞節がきている。In seeing は「…見るときには」という意味の副詞句として用いられている。また，with は「…を用いて」という意味であり，前置詞＋名詞に続く alone は「…だけ」という意味を表す。

例　He can't live on his small salary alone.

「彼はわずかな給料だけでは生活が成り立たない」

□ immediately「すぐ近くに」

問4 空所(4)を含む文に続いて，「草の上を転がっている犬に触れることで，その犬と心を通わせることができた」というヘレン・ケラーの日記が引用されていることから，「犬に触れることでありふれた経験に新たな感覚が生じる」とわかる。

ア.「ありふれた」イ.「わくわくするような」ウ.「危険な」エ.「恐ろしい」

問5 空所(5)を含む文に続いて，「驚くほど発達した触覚」の具体例が3つ述べられている。

ア.「基本的な区別」イ.「驚くべき発達」ウ.「感情的な経験」エ.「神秘的な予言」

問6 be aware of A「Aに気づいている」の A の位置に疑問詞 how で導かれた名詞節がきている。また，how important は，be important to A の important が how と結びついたもの。

□ complete「完全な」

問7 本文全体を通して，触れることの重要性が述べられている。

ア.「どうぞお好きなように」イ.「跳ぶ前に見よ」ウ.「あきらめてはいけない」
エ.「どうぞ触れてみてください」

Advice 具体例，体験談，引用

英文中に出てくる具体例，体験談，引用は，読み手に対して筆者が何かを説得力を持って言うために使われる。したがって，これらが何を言うためのものなのかを確認することが，論旨の展開，さらには文の内容を把握するうえで大切である。本問の第1段落中のマーク・トウェインの引用，第2～4段落中の筆者の体験談は「触れることの重要性」を言うためのものである。また，問4は第5段落中のヘレン・ケラーの日記からの引用が，問5は第6段落中の具体例がそれぞれ何を言うためのものなのかを読み取らせる問題である。

要　約

見るだけではなく，触れることで対象となるものを深く理解することができる。今日では触れることの重要性が理解されるようになってきている。(66字)

構文・語句解説

第1・2段落

[1]"Don't look at the world with your hands in your pockets," Mark Twain once told an aspiring young author. [2]"To write about it you have to reach out and touch it."

[3]I thought of this advice when I visited Robert Barnett, former executive director of the American Foundation for the Blind. [4]Barnett was blinded at the age of 14 in an accident. [5]As we chatted, he noticed, I don't know how, that I was gazing at a life-size bronze head of Helen Keller, which he keeps near his desk.

[1]「ポケットに手を入れたまま世の中を見てはいけない」マーク・トウェインはかつて成功することを願っている若い作家に語った。[2]「世の中について書くためには，手を伸ばして触れてみる必要がある」

[3]米国盲人連盟の前理事長のロバート・バーネットを訪問したとき，私はこのアドバイスを思い出した。[4]バーネットは14歳のときに事故で失明した。[5]談笑していると，彼の机の近くに置いてあったヘレン・ケラーの等身大のブロンズ製の頭像を私が見つめていることに，どうしてかはわからないが，彼は気づいたのである。

1 with your hands in your pockets は付帯状況の with を用いた表現。with A ～ で「Aが～の状態で」という意味。

□ aspiring「成功することを願っている，大志を抱いている」

2 □ reach out「手を伸ばす」

3 □ think of A「Aを思い出す」　□ former「前の」　□ executive director「理事長」

4 □ be blinded「失明する」

5 I don't know how は he noticed that I ... という主節に対して，注釈的な情報を述べたもの。

□ chat「談笑する」　□ notice「に気づく」　□ gaze at A「Aを見つめる」

□ life-size「実物大の」　□ head「頭像」

第3～5段落

[1]"Feel it with your hands," he told me. [2]I ran my fingers over the cool metal. [3]"Now does it look any different?" Barnett asked.

[4]The difference was surprising. [5]The sculpture now had weight, depth, shape and character which had escaped my eyes.

[6]"Touch is more than a substitute for vision," Barnett said. [7]"It reveals qualities other senses can't even suggest. [8]One of the greatest mistakes people make is thinking you have to be blind to enjoy it." [9]Learning to develop the sense of touch is something like making your other senses secondary. [10]In seeing with the eyes alone we are limited to what is immediately in front of us. [11]Touch along with vision enables us to see something as a whole.

[1]「手で触ってみてください」彼は私に言った。[2]私は冷たい金属の上に指を滑らした。[3]「さあ，何か違いは見えませんか」バーネットは尋ねた。

[4]その違いは驚くべきものだった。[5]今やその塑像には，眼ではとらえられなかった重さ，深

さ，形，個性があった。

[6]「触れることは視覚の代わり以上のものなのです」とバーネットは言った。[7]「それは他の感覚では思い起こさせることもできない様々な特色をあらわにするのです。[8]人が犯す最も大きな間違いの１つは，それを楽しむには盲目でなければならないと考えることです」[9]触覚を発達させられるようになることは，他の感覚を副次的なものにすることといくらか似ている。[10]目だけを使って見るときには，私たちはまさに目の前にあるものだけに限られてしまう。[11]見ることに加えて触れることで，私たちは全体として何かを見ることができるのである。

2 □ run「を走らせる」

5 which had escaped my eyes は weight, depth, shape and character を修飾する関係代名詞節。

□ sculpture「塑像，彫刻」　□ character「個性」　□ escape「を逃れる」

6 □ more than A「A以上のもの」　□ substitute for A「Aに代わるもの」

□ vision「視覚，視力」

7 other senses can't even suggest は qualities を修飾する関係代名詞節。

□ reveal「を明らかにする」　□ suggest「を示唆する」

8 One of ... is thinking は One が主語，is が述語動詞，thinking 以下が補語となる動名詞句。people make は the greatest mistake を修飾する関係代名詞節。

9 □ learn to *do*「…できるようになる」　□ be something like A「いくぶんAに似ている」

□ secondary「副次的な，二次的な」

11 □ along with A「Aに加えて」　□ enable O to *do*「Oが…することを可能にする」

□ as a whole「全体として」

第６段落

[1]Awareness of touch can bring a new feeling to the most commonplace experiences. [2]"I have just touched my dog," wrote the young Helen Keller in her diary. [3]"He was rolling on the grass with pleasure in every muscle and limb. [4]I wanted to catch a picture of him in my fingers, and I touched him lightly as I would cobwebs. [5]But, to my surprise, his body turned towards me and moved into a sitting position, and his tongue gave my hand a lick. [6]He pressed close to me as if he intended to put himself into my hand. [7]He loved it with his tail, with his paw, with his tongue. [8]If he could speak I believe he would say with me that paradise is attained by touch."

[1]触れることを意識することで最もありふれた経験に新たな感覚が生じることがある。[2]若き日のヘレン・ケラーは日記に記している。「私は犬に触れたところだ。[3]その犬はすべての筋肉と足で喜びを表しながら，草の上を転がっていた。[4]私は指の中にその犬の姿をとらえたかったので，クモの巣に触れるように軽く触れてみた。[5]しかし驚いたことに，その犬は身体を私の方に向けて，おすわりの姿勢になり，舌で私の手をなめた。[6]まるで私の手の中に入るつもりであるかのように，身体をぐっと押し付けてきた。[7]尻尾で，足で，舌で，そうするのを楽しんでいた。[8]その犬が話すことができたら，楽園は触れることで得られる，と私と一緒に言うのではないかと思う」

1 □ awareness「意識」

3 □ muscle「筋肉」　□ limb「〈頭部・胴体と区別して〉肢体，手足」

4 as I would cobwebs = as I would touch cobwebs

□ picture「心に描くもの，理解」　□ cobweb「クモの巣」

5 □ to A's surprise「Aが驚いたことに」　□ sitting position「おすわりの姿勢」

□ tongue「舌」　□ give A a lick「Aをなめる」

6 □ press「押す」　□ close to A「Aにぴったりと」　□ as if S V ...「まるで…のように」

□ intend to *do*「…するつもりである」

7 □ tail「尻尾」　□ paw「〈犬・猫などの〉足」

8 If he could speak I believe he would say ... の If 節は he would say ... に対する仮定法の条件節。

□ paradise「楽園」　□ attain「を獲得する」

第7段落

[1]The sense of touch is capable of extraordinary development. [2]Expert millers can recognize any grade of flour by rubbing a little between thumb and forefinger. [3]A cloth expert can identify the coloring used in a cloth by the difference it makes in the texture. [4]The blind botanist, John Grimshaw Wilkinson, learned to distinguish more than 5,000 species of plants by touching them lightly with his tongue.

[1]触覚は驚くほど発達することもある。[2]熟練した粉引き職人は，親指と人差し指の間で少しこするだけでどんな小麦粉の等級も識別できる。[3]布地の専門家は，肌触りの違いで布地に使われている染料を特定できる。[4]盲目の植物学者，ジョン・グリムショー・ウィルキンソンは，舌で軽く触れるだけで5,000種以上の植物を区別できるようになった。

1 □ be capable of A「Aの可能性がある」

2 □ expert「熟練した／専門家」 □ miller「粉屋，製粉業者」 □ recognize「を識別する」
□ grade「等級」 □ flour「小麦粉」 □ rub「をこする」 □ thumb「親指」
□ forefinger「人差し指」

3 it makes 以下は the difference を修飾する関係代名詞節。
□ identify「を特定する」 □ coloring「染料」 □ texture「肌触り，手触り」

4 □ botanist「植物学者」 □ distinguish「を区別する」 □ species「種」

第8・9段落

[1]We are aware today of how important touch is to complete understanding of anything, and there are now museums that, instead of the old "Don't Touch" signs, offer children the chance to touch — to feel the roundness of a sculpture, the beautiful balance of an Inca pitcher, and the rough iron of an early New England kettle. [2]Visitors to the Brooklyn Children's Museum are encouraged to pick up and handle the objects on display in every exhibit. [3]"If they can't touch the things," says Michael Cohn, the museum's senior instructor of anthropology, "it is no different from watching a movie or TV show."

[4]Maybe, as we all aim to enlarge the range of our impressions, our motto should be: Do touch!

[1]今日私たちは，どんなものでも完全に理解するのに触れることがいかに重要であるのかに気づいているし，今では，昔からある「手を触れないでください」という掲示の代わりに，子供たちに触れる機会を，彫刻の丸みや，インカの水差しの見事な均整，初期のニューイングランドのやかんのざらざらした鉄を感じる機会を与える博物館もある。[2]ブルックリン子供博物館を訪れる人は，すべての展示で陳列されているものを手にとって，触れてみるように勧められる。[3]「もしも触ることができなければ，映画やテレビ番組を見るのとまったく変わりませんよ」と，この博物館の人類学上級指導員のマイケル・コーンは言っている。

[4]おそらく，印象の幅を広げることを誰もが目指す以上は，私たちのモットーは当然次のようなものになるだろう。「どうぞ触れてみてください」

1 □ instead of A「Aの代わりに」 □ the chance to *do*「する機会」 □ roundness「丸み」
□ Inca「インカの」 □ pitcher「水差し」 □ rough「ざらざらした」 □ iron「鉄」

2 the objects は pick up と handle に共通する目的語。
□ encourage O to *do*「Oに…するように勧める，促す」 □ pick A up「Aを手にとる」
□ handle「に手で触れる」 □ object「物」 □ on display「陳列された」

□ exhibit「展示」

3 □ senior instructor「上級指導員」　□ anthropology「人類学」

4 □ aim to *do*「…することを目指す」　□ enlarge「を広げる」　□ range「範囲」

□ motto「モットー，標語」

13 移動の意味

解答

問1　(1a)　イ．virtual　(1b)　ウ．previous　(1c)　ア．opposite
(1d)　エ．spiritual

問2　ウ．先々のことは考えないで

問3　ア．time

問4　価値観や当然とされていることが地域によって違うこと。(26字)

問5　旅するときに私たちが見つけるものは何であれ，いつも心の中に持っていたものにすぎないのだ。

問6　イ

設問解説

問1　(1a) 空所を含む文の主語 Global communications「地球規模の通信網」とは第1段落第4文の具体例からしてもインターネットのことである。「インターネットがすべての人をどのような隣人にしたのか」を考える。

(1b) 第3段落第1・2文で「変化があまりに急速であり，過去が未来の準備にならない」と述べている。「導いてくれるどのような例がないのか」を考える。

(1c) 第4段落第1文では「今では時間を超えて旅することができる」ということが述べられている。「今夜にはどのような季節の真っ只中へ飛んで行くこともできるか」を考える。

(1d) 第5段落第3文では「価値観が混乱する」ということが述べられている。「明日の旅は，どのような混乱という感覚を伴うものなのか」を考える。

ア.「反対の」イ.「実質的な」ウ.「以前の」エ.「精神的な」

問2　下線部(2)の文字通りの意味は「道の曲がり角を数えることなく」である。これは，第2段落第1文の we fail sometimes to consider where we are going or what we might be losing を比喩的に述べたもの。

□ count「を数える」　□ bend「曲がり角，曲がったもの」

問3　able 以下で，「21世紀から13世紀へと」，つまり「現在から過去へと」時間旅行することができると述べている。

問4　下線部(4)を含む文は「空間的な距離が縮まることで，私たちは今なお残るより意味のある距離が見えなくなっているのかもしれない」という意味。コロン以下の flying from Beirut to Beijing to Bogota on successive days とは「空間的な距離が縮まること」を具体的に述べ，we may underestimate the differences in values and assumptions と続いている。また，次の文ではこの内容を「村の広場で正しいとされることが地球村の隅々にまで行き渡ることはない」と比喩的に述べている。したがって，「今なお残るより意味のある距離」とは「価値観や当然とされていることが地域によって違うこと」である。

□ significant「意義深い」

問 5 whatever we ... we travel が述語動詞 is の主語となる名詞節。whatever に導かれた節が名詞節になるときは「…する何でも，…するどんなものも」，副詞節になるときは「たとえ何が[を]…しても」という意味。また，関係代名詞 what で導かれた名詞節が補語である。

例 1 He tells us whatever happens.
「彼は私たちに起きることは何でも話してくれる」

例 2 We will love you whatever happens.
「何が起きても私たちはあなたのことを愛しています」

□ all along「ずっと，初めから」

問 6 ア.「家にいては世界中の文化を楽しむことはできない」第 2 段落第 1 文の内容に不一致。

イ.「今日のような国境のない時代には根なし草の人が増えている」第 2 段落の内容に一致。

ウ.「テレビを見るとき，次々と変わる画像が世界の優れた理解を与えてくれる」第 5 段落第 1 文の内容に不一致。

エ.「エマソンは，旅することで人々の心が豊かになると考えた」第 5 段落第 5 文の内容に不一致。

Advice 比喩表現

比喩表現は，何かを説明するときに他の物事を借りて表現するものである。比喩表現を文字通り解釈しただけでは，筆者が何を言おうとしているのかわからないことも多い。文章中の具体的に述べられた部分から，何を言うための比喩なのかを確認することが大切である。また，比喩表現が，説明問題や選択問題で問われることも多い。本問では，問 2，問 3 の該当箇所をはじめ，比喩表現が多用されている。

要　約

移動手段や通信網の発達によって，物理的距離は縮まっているが，地域間の価値観の違いが

見えなくなり，しっかりした拠りどころのない者にとってはいっそうの精神的混乱が生じる恐れがある。(88字)

構文・語句解説

第1段落

[1]All of us, almost daily, experience the mobility of our world: we could be in Tibet tomorrow. [2]And not only our bodies, but also our minds are traveling at the speed of light. [3]Global communications have made us all virtual neighbors and taught us tolerance. [4]Two generations ago, there were no roads in Nepal; now the information superhighway and English language paths run through the teahouses of the Himalayas.

[1]誰もが，毎日のように，私たちの世界の移動性を経験している。明日にはチベットにいるかもしれないのである。[2]それに，肉体だけでなく精神も光速で移動している。[3]地球規模の通信網によって，あらゆる人が実質的に隣人となり，私たちは寛大であることを学んだ。[4]2世代前には，ネパールに道路はなかったが，今では情報スーパーハイウェイと英語の小道がヒマラヤ山地の茶店にまで通っている。

1 □ mobility「あちこち移動できること，移動性」

2 □ not only X but also Y「XだけでなくYも」

3 □ global「地球規模の，世界的な」　□ communications「通信網，通信機関」

□ tolerance「寛大さ，容認」

4 □ information superhighway「情報スーパーハイウェイ」インターネットのこと。

□ run through A「〈道などが〉Aを通って伸びている」　□ the Himalayas「ヒマラヤ山脈」

第2段落

[1]Yet even as we enjoy the opportunities of the borderless economy and the varieties of world music and our ability to appreciate the cultures of the world in our living rooms, we fail sometimes to consider where we are going or what we might be losing. [2]"To be rooted," wrote the philosopher Simone Weil, "is perhaps the most important and least recognized need of the human soul." [3]And in our dawning age of rootlessness, we tend to speed into the future without counting the bends in the road.

[1]しかしながら，私たちが，国境のない経済の機会を享受し，様々なワールドミュージックを

楽しみ，世界中の文化を居間にいながら楽しめるときでさえも，自分たちがどこに向かおうとしているのか，何を失いかけているのかをときおり考えてみることもない。²哲学者のシモーヌ・ヴェーユは記した。「根を下ろしていることは，おそらく，人間の魂が必要としている最も重要で，かつ最も認められていないものである」と。³そして，今始まろうとしている根なし草の時代に，私たちは道にある曲がり角を数えることもなく，未来へと突き進みがちなのである。

1 □ borderless「国境のない」　□ variety「多様性」

□ world music「ワールドミュージック」第三世界のエスニックな色彩の強いポピュラーミュージックのこと。

□ A's ability to *do*「Aが…できること」　□ appreciate「を正しく認識する，味わう」

□ fail to *do*「…しない，できない」

2 □ be rooted「根を下ろしている」　□ recognized「(社会的に)認められた」

3 □ dawning「今始まろうとしている／夜明け」

□ rootlessness「根なし草であること，社会的立場がないこと」

□ tend to *do*「…しがちである」　□ speed into A「Aへと突き進む」

第3段落

¹One problem, of course, is that everything is happening so quickly. ²Five years ago is ancient history now, and yesterday scarcely prepares us for today. ³We have no previous examples to guide us. ⁴The classical poets Homer and Virgil sang of travelers, but not ones crossing 11 time zones before noon. ⁵And nomads have always traveled across the earth, but on foot and in tune with the rhythm of the seasons and tradition. ⁶A new age of mobility means a new age of homesickness—and that is for those of us lucky enough to have a home.

¹問題の1つは，言うまでもなく，すべてがあまりにも急速に起きているということである。²5年前が今では古代史であり，昨日が今日の準備にはまずならない。³私たちには導いてくれる先例がないのである。⁴古典詩人のホメロスやウェルギリウスは旅人について詠んだが，正午までに時間帯を11も横断する旅人については詠んでいない。⁵また遊牧民はいつも大地をあちこち移動してきたが，徒歩で，しかも季節や伝統のリズムに合わせて移動してきたのである。⁶移動性の新時代とはホームシックの新時代のことである。ただし，幸運にも家を持っている人にだけ言えることではあるが。

2 Five years ago が is の主語として用いられている。

□ ancient history「古代史」　□ scarcely「ほとんど…ない」

□ prepare A for B「AにBの準備をさせる」

3 □ guide「を導く」

4 but not ones crossing ... =but did not sing of ones crossing ... なお，crossing ... 以下は ones を修飾する現在分詞句で，ones は travelers の代用。

□ classical「〈古代ギリシア・ローマの〉古典の」　□ Homer「ホメロス」

□ Virgil「ウェルギリウス」　□ time zone「〈同一標準時を用いる〉時間帯」

5 but on foot ... =but have traveled on foot ...

□ earth「陸地」　□ on foot「徒歩で」　□ in tune with A「Aと調子が合って」

□ rhythm「リズム」　□ tradition「伝統」

6 that is for those of us lucky enough to have a home の that はダッシュの前の文の内容を指している。lucky 以下は those を修飾する形容詞句で those は「人々」という意味。

第4段落

[1]All of us are time travelers now, able to fly in less than a day from the 21st century (downtown Tokyo, for example) to the 13th (Bhutan, where costumes, houses and customs are maintained in strict medieval style). [2]Tonight we can fly into the depths of the opposite season — or into the arms of a family we have not seen for 20 years. [3]And the shrinking of distances in space may blind us to the more significant distances that remain: flying from Beirut to Beijing to Bogota on successive days — and finding the same services in each — we may underestimate the differences in values and assumptions. [4]The truths of the village square do not extend across the global village.

[1]今や誰もが時間旅行者であり，24時間以内に21世紀(たとえば，東京の繁華街)から13世紀(衣服や家屋，習慣が厳密に中世の様式で維持されているブータン)まで飛ぶことができる。[2]今夜には反対の季節の真っ只中へも，また20年間会わなかった家族の腕の中へも飛んで行くことができる。[3]そして，空間的な距離が縮まることで，私たちは今なお残るより意味のある距離が見えなくなっているのかもしれない。ベイルートから北京へ，さらにボゴタへと連日飛び，それぞれの場所で同じサービスを受けることで，価値観や当然とされていることの違いを軽んじているのかもしれない。[4]村の広場で正しいとされることが地球村の隅々にまで行き渡ることはない。

1 able 以下は are time travelers に対する補足説明。

□ Bhutan「ブータン」インド北東部，ヒマラヤ山脈中の王国。　□ strict「厳密な」

☐ medieval「中世の」

2 we have not seen for 20 years は a family を修飾する関係代名詞節。

☐ depth「真最中」

3 ☐ shrinking「縮小，縮み」　☐ blind A to B「AにBを見えなくする」

☐ Beirut「ベイルート」レバノンの首都。　☐ Beijing「北京」中華人民共和国の首都。

☐ Bogota「ボゴタ」コロンビアの首都。　☐ successive「連続した」

☐ underestimate「を軽んじる，過小評価する」　☐ values「価値観」

☐ assumption「当然とされていること，想定」

4 ☐ village square「村の広場」　☐ extend「広がる，届く」

☐ global village「地球村」情報の共有化などによって1つの村のようになった地球のこと。

第5段落

[1]Thus traveling today can be like watching TV, channel surfing through a mass of images too fast to read and too various to sort. [2]And traveling tomorrow, for those of us without a firm sense of neighborhood or community or home, may involve an even stronger sense of spiritual confusion. [3]Our values like our bodies may be up in the air or lost in space. [4]The only thing that can support the burden of our movement, after all, is a steadying sense of stillness. [5]"Though we travel the world over to find the beautiful, we must carry it with us or we find it not," wrote the philosopher Emerson, who considered travel a "fool's paradise." [6]The same is even truer of our sense of destination or home: whatever we find when we travel is only what we had inside us all along.

[1]こうして，今日の旅はテレビを見ること，チャンネルを次々に換えてあまりに速すぎて読むことも，あまりに多様で分類することもできない大量の画像を見ることに似ている。[2]そして明日の旅は，近隣や地域社会，自分が本来いるべきところというしっかりした感覚を持たない者にとっては，精神的混乱というさらに強い感覚を伴うものかもしれない。[3]肉体同様私たちの価値観は宙に漂い，空間に消えてしまうことになるかもしれない。[4]そもそも，移動という負担を支えてくれるものは，静止しているという安定感だけなのである。[5]「私たちは美しいものを見つけようと世界中を旅しているが，美しいものは携えていなければならないし，そうでなければ見つかることはない」と，旅とは「愚か者の楽園」であると考えた哲学者のエマソンは記した。[6]同じことは，旅先あるいは自分が本来いるべきところにいるという私たちの感覚にさらに当てはまる。旅するときに私たちが見つけるものは何であれ，いつも心の中に持っていたものにすぎないのだ。

1 too fast to read and too various to sort は a mass of images を修飾する形容詞句で，too ... to *do*「あまりに…なので～できない」の表現が用いられている。

□ channel surfing「テレビのチャンネルを次々に切り換えること」

□ a mass of A「大量のA」　□ various「様々な」　□ sort「を分類する」

2 □ firm「しっかりした」　□ community「地域社会」

□ home「自分が本来いるべきところ」今住んでいる場所や生まれた場所のことで，そこに属していることを強調して用いられている。

□ involve「を伴う」　□ confusion「混乱」

3 □ up in the air「宙に漂って」

4 □ burden「負担，重荷」　□ after all「そもそも，何と言っても…だから」

□ a steadying sense「安定感」　□ stillness「静止」

5 we find it not は古い英語で，we don't find it と同意。

□ travel A over「Aをあちこち旅する」　□ the beautiful「美しいもの」

□ carry A with *one*「Aを持ち歩く，携行する」　□ paradise「楽園」

6 □ even＋比較級「さらに…，いっそう…」　□ be true of A「Aに当てはまる」

□ destination「旅先，目的地」

14 左脳と右脳

解答

問1　この能力が行動や世界の解釈の仕方における非対称につながることがある。

問2　(2a) エ. less　(2b) ウ. Similarly　(2c) イ. dull

問3　ウ

問4　被験者たちは，伝えられる内容と声の調子の両方の点から文の感情的内容を分類するよう求められる。

問5　左耳による判断がより優れている傾向が少しでもあれば，それはその作業に右半球がより多く関わっている証拠と解釈される。

問6　(6a) left　(6b) right　(6c) right

設問解説

問1　These は前文の different cognitive capacities を指す。in behavior と in the way in which we interpret the world が and で結ばれている。in which 以下は the way を修飾する関係代名詞節。なお，can は可能性を表しているので，「…することがある／…しかねない」と訳出する。

□ lead to A「Aに通じる，つながる」　□ asymmetry「非対称」　□ behavior「行動」　□ interpret「を解釈する」

問2　(2a) 前の文にある some sentences と比べて，空所(2a)を含む文の other sentences がどのような内容の文なのかに注目する。「賞を取った」とか「太陽が輝いている」という文に比べて「ギャンブルで金をすった」とか「雨が激しく降っている」という文は「暗い内容」の文であることがわかるので，「前の文ほど cheerful でない」という意味になるようにする。

ア.「極めて…」 イ.「より…」 ウ.「同じだけ…」 エ.「より…でない」

(2b) 空所を含む文の末尾に，前の文で使われている in a cheerful tone of voice という表現があることに注目する。この2文ではどちらも「普通は暗い内容の文でも，場合によって明るく読まれることがある」という内容を表しているので，ウが正解。

ア.「しかし」 イ.「そうではなくて」 ウ.「同様に」 エ.「したがって」

(2c) 空所を含む文では，「脳に損傷を受けた患者の発話内容は感情的に起伏がなく，損傷を受ける前のようなふさわしい変化や抑揚を欠いている」と述べた後で「そういった発話がどのように聞こえるのか」を述べている。次の文で「実際，言語のより創造的な要素が欠落していることがうかがえる」と述べられていることから判断する。

ア.「おもしろい」イ.「単調な」ウ.「感情の」エ.「正常な」

問3 下線部(3)は「文は様々な声の調子で読まれるが，その調子は文の内容に一致していたり反していたりする」という意味である。したがって，「内容に関わりなく明るい調子で読まれたり，暗い調子で読まれたりする」ことになるので，ウが正解。なお，which 以下は different tones of voice を補足説明する非制限用法の関係代名詞節。

□ different A「様々なA」　□ tone「調子，トーン」

□ either X or Y「XかYのいずれか」

□ be consistent with A「Aと一致している，矛盾しない」

□ in opposition to A「Aと対立して」

問4 全体の文の構造は，ask O to *do*「Oに…するように求める」が受動態になったもの。ここでの主語の Subjects は「被験者，実験対象」という意味であることに注意。both 以下は categorize を修飾する副詞句で，both X and Y「XとYの両方とも」の X に in terms of the message that is conveyed，Y に (in terms of) the tone of voice がきていると考えるとよい。なお，that is conveyed は the message を修飾する関係代名詞節。

□ categorize「を分類する」　□ emotional「感情の，情緒の」　□ content「内容」

□ in terms of A「Aの観点から」　□ convey「を伝える」

問5 全体の文の構造は take O as C「OをCだとみなす，解釈する」が受動態になったもの。bias towards A で「Aへの傾向，偏り」という意味だが，ここでは superior judgments from the left ear が A となっている。increased right-hemisphere involvement は，「増加した右半球の関わり」が直訳であるが，「右半球の関わりが増えること」とするとより自然な訳になる。

□ any A「〈肯定文で〉どんなAでも」　□ superior「より優れている」

□ judgment「判断」　□ evidence「証拠」　□ involvement in A「Aとの関わり」

□ task「作業」

問6 空所(6a)(6b)を含む文は「この種の実験では，(　6a　)の耳の方が声の調子を判断するのに優れており，(　6b　)の耳の方が言葉の中身を判断するのに優れている」という意味である。第2段落第1文には，脳の右半球は「話をする際の声の感情的な調子を解釈するのがうまい」とあり，第3段落第3文には「左耳が脳の右半球とより密接に関連している」とあるので，「左耳の方が声の調子に関する判断が優れている」ことになる。したがって，(6a)には left が入る。また，それと対比的になる(6b)には right が入る。

空所(6c)を含む文は「(　6c　)半球に損傷を受け脳に障害を負った患者は，そのように話し言葉から感情の状態を解釈することに苦労する」という意味である。第2段落第1文および第4段落第4文から，話し言葉から感情の調子を判断するのが優れているのは脳の右半球であることがわかるので，(6c)には right が入る。

Advice 実験・調査の紹介

論説文でも特に自然科学や心理学など理系のトピックを扱った文章では，筆者がある事実を裏づけるために，実験や調査などを紹介することが多い。このような場合，その実験・調査の「方法」，「結果」を正確に読み取る必要がある。本問では，「脳の右半球の方が発話の中の感情を解釈するのに優れている」ことを裏づける実験が第2・3段落で紹介されており，問3が実験の「方法」を，問6が実験の「結果」について，内容の理解を問うている。

要　約

人間の脳は左半球と右半球で認識機能が異なっていて，そのために行動や世界の解釈の仕方が異なるようである。実験などから，右半球の方が左半球よりも発話の中の感情を解釈するのに優れていることがわかっている。(99字)

▶▶▶ 構文・語句解説 ◀◀◀

第1段落

[1]We know that the two cerebral hemispheres of the brain have different cognitive capacities. [2]These can lead to asymmetries in behavior and in the way in which we interpret the world. [3]Many studies suggest that the right hemisphere of the brain is more involved in the perception of emotion and in its expression than the left hemisphere of the brain.

[1]脳の2つの大脳半球が異なる認識能力を持っていることを私たちは知っている。[2]この能力が行動や世界の解釈の仕方における非対称につながることがある。[3]脳の右半球が左半球よりも感情の認識や表現により多く関与していることを多くの研究が示唆している。

1 □ capacity「能力」

3 □ study「研究，調査」 □ suggest that 節「…ということを示唆する」

□ be involved in A「A に関わっている」 □ perception「認識，理解」

□ emotion「感情，情緒」 □ expression「表現」

第 2 段落

[1]In relation to language, the right hemisphere of the brain is better at interpreting the emotional tone of voice in speech. [2]A typical experiment illustrates this. [3]It uses some sentences with a happy message like "She won a prize" or "The sun is shining." [4]Other sentences are less cheerful; "He lost all his money gambling" or "It is raining very heavily," and yet other sentences are neutral with no particular emotional content. [5]They are read in different tones of voice, which are either consistent with the sentence's message or in opposition to it. [6]Although in principle to lose money gambling is unpleasant, if it had happened to a great enemy it might nevertheless induce some sensation of pleasure, and it is possible to read the sentence "He lost all his money gambling" in a cheerful tone of voice. [7]Similarly, some Californians have an unusual enthusiasm for rain and it is possible to read the sentence "It is cold and rainy" in a cheerful tone of voice.

[1]言語に関しては，脳の右半球の方が，話をする際の声の感情的な調子を解釈するのがうまい。[2]典型的な実験がこのことを例証している。[3]実験には「彼女が賞をとったよ」とか「太陽が輝いている」といった明るい伝達内容を持った文がいくつか使われる。[4]他には「彼はギャンブルで金を全部すってしまった」とか「雨がとても激しく降っている」といった，それほど楽しくない内容の文もあるし，さらにまた特に感情的な内容を持たない中立的な文もある。[5]これらの文は様々な声の調子で読まれるが，その調子は文の伝達内容に一致していたり反していたりする。[6]ギャンブルでお金を失うことは原則として不愉快なことだが，それにもかかわらず，それがひどく敵対関係にある人に起きたとすれば，何らかの快感を引き出すかもしれず，「彼はギャンブルで金を全部すってしまった」という文を明るい声の調子で読むこともできる。[7]同様に，カリフォルニアに住む人の中には雨に対して珍しいほど強い関心を持っている人がいて，「寒いし雨がよく降るね」という文を明るい声の調子で読むこともできる。

1 □ in relation to A「A に関して」

□ be good at *doing*「…するのが上手である，得意である」 □ speech「話し言葉／発話」

2 □ typical「典型的な」 □ experiment「実験」 □ illustrate「を説明する，例証する」

3 □ prize「賞」

4 □ cheerful「楽しい，楽観的な」　□ lose O（in）*doing*「…してOを浪費する」

□ gamble「ギャンブルをする」　□ heavily「〈雨が〉激しく，多量に」

□ yet other A「さらに他のA」　□ neutral「中立的な」　□ particular「特別な」

6 Although 節内では to lose money gambling が主語となっている。

if it ... of pleasure において，if it ... great enemy が仮定法過去完了の条件節，it might ... of pleasure が仮定法過去の帰結節となっている。

□ in principle「原則として」　□ unpleasant「不愉快な，楽しくない」

□ happen to A「〈出来事などが〉Aに起きる，生じる」　□ enemy「敵対関係にある人」

□ nevertheless「それにもかかわらず」　□ induce「を誘引する，誘発する」

□ sensation「感情」

7 □ similarly「同様に」　□ Californian「カリフォルニアの人」

□ unusual「珍しいほどの，まれな」　□ enthusiasm「強い関心，熱意」

第3段落

[1]Subjects are asked to categorize the emotional content of the sentence both in terms of the message that is conveyed and the tone of voice. [2]Two sentences are presented at the same moment, one played to the right ear and one played to the left ear, in a listening set-up. [3]Since the connections that the left ear makes with the right hemisphere are stronger than the connections the right ear makes with the right hemisphere, any bias towards superior judgments from the left ear is taken as evidence of increased right-hemisphere involvement in the task. [4]In this kind of experiment, the left ear is better at making judgments about the tone of voice, whereas the right ear is better at judging verbal content.

[1]被験者たちは，伝えられる内容と声の調子の両方の点から文の感情的内容を分類するよう求められる。[2]2つの文がリスニング用の装置で同時に提示され，1つは右の耳に1つは左の耳に聞こえるようにしてある。[3]左耳が右半球と作っている関係の方が右耳が右半球と作っている関係よりも強いので，左耳による判断がより優れている傾向が少しでもあれば，それはその作業に右半球がより多く関わっている証拠と解釈される。[4]この種の実験では，左耳の方が声の調子を判断するのに優れているのに対して，右耳の方が言葉の中身を判断するのに優れている。

2 one played ... left ear は付帯状況の分詞構文。one は one of the two sentences の意味。

□ present「を提示する」　□ listening set-up「リスニング用の装置，設備」

3 □ connection「関係」

4 □ whereas S V ...「ところが一方…」　□ verbal「言葉の」

第４段落

[1]Brain-damaged patients who have sustained injuries to the right hemisphere have difficulty in making such interpretations of emotional mood from speech. [2]Their language and communicative systems appear relatively normal, in terms of being able to say roughly what they want to say, but the content of their speech is often emotionally flat, lacking its previous variation and modulation and sounding rather dull. [3]In fact, it is suggested that the more creative elements in language are absent. [4]Some of the connotative associations of language may be influenced by the right hemisphere.

[1]右半球に損傷を受け脳に障害を負った患者は，そのように話し言葉から感情の状態を解釈することに苦労する。[2]こうした患者の言語と伝達の体系は，自分の言いたいことを大まかには言うことができるという点では比較的正常なように見えるが，発話の内容は感情的に起伏がないことが多く，損傷を受ける前のような変化や抑揚を欠き，かなり単調に聞こえる。[3]実際，言語のより創造的な要素が欠落していることがうかがえる。[4]言外の意味の連想の一部は右半球に影響されているかもしれない。

1 □ brain-damaged「脳に損傷を負った」　□ patient「患者」
□ sustain「〈損害・傷害など〉を被る，受ける／を維持する」　□ injury「けが」
□ have difficulty in *doing*「…するのに苦労する」　□ interpretation「解釈」
□ mood「気分」

2 lacking its ... and modulation と sounding rather dull の２つの分詞構文が and で結ばれている。
□ communicative「意思伝達の，コミュニケーションの」
□ appear C「Cのように見える，思える」　□ relatively「比較的，相対的に」
□ roughly「大ざっぱに，おおまかに」　□ flat「起伏のない」　□ lack「を欠く」
□ previous「以前の」　□ variation「変化」　□ sound C「Cのように聞こえる」

3 □ in fact「実際，実は」　□ creative「創造的な」　□ element「要素」
□ absent「ない，欠けている」

4 □ association「連想」　□ influence「に影響する」

15 妻の介護

解答

問1　彼は学長になったとき，自分は神によって命じられたのであり，自分はその地位にふさわしいのだ，と確信した。

問2　妻がアルツハイマー病の兆候を見せ始めたこと。(22字)

問3　妻の介護のために学長の職を辞すること。(19字)

問4　約束は仕事よりも重要であるということ。(19字)

問5　イ．interfere with

問6　彼は現実主義者たちに，今では物忘れがひどい彼女の中に自分が何年も前に結婚した同じすてきな女性を認められる，とわかってもらった。

問7　ア

設問解説

問1 be convinced that 節「…だと確信する」の that 節内において，was called ... と was worthy ... が and で結ばれている。ここでの call は「〈神が〉〈天職に〉召す」という意味である。また，that position とは the president の地位を指している。

□ president「学長」　□ be worthy of A「Aに値する」

問2 tragedy は「悲劇」という意味。その内容は続く第4段落第2文 His wife ... Alzheimer's disease. に述べられている。

問3 下線部(3)は「彼がやろうとしていること」という意味。第5～7段落第1文に「彼は決意した」とあり，続く第2文に，その決意の内容が具体的に述べられている。

問4 下線部(4)は「彼(マックウィルキン)は神がやるように命じたことから去ろうとしている，と言う信心深い人」という意味である。このような人たちに対するロバートソン・マックウィルキンの答えは，第8・9段落第6文コロン(：)以下に述べられている。There is ... a promise. を制限字数に留意してまとめる。

□ religious「信心深い」　□ call O to *do*「Oに…するように命じる，召す」

問5 空所(5)の直前に「彼(マックウィルキン)は神がやるように命じたことから去ろうとしている，と言う信心深い人もいた」と述べられている。したがって，「彼の妻に対する気遣いという私的なことが，社会的責任をどのようなものにすれば，信心深い人たちの主張にあうのか」を考えればよい。したがって，イが正解。

ア.「に専念する」 イ.「を妨げる」 ウ.「に役立つ」 エ.「を取り上げる」

問6 主語の he は同じ第8・9段落第1文の The man つまり Robertson McQuilken を指す。let O know は「Oに…を知らせる」という意味なので，「彼(マックウィルキン)は彼らにわかってもらった」となる。したがって，them とはマックウィルキンが答えた相手，つまり第8・9段落第2文の the realists を指す。that he ... years ago は know の目的語となる名詞節であり，その節内は he(S) recognized(V) the same lovely woman(O) という構造。また，he had ... years ago は woman を修飾する関係代名詞節。

□ recognize「を認める，を(それと)識別する」　□ now-forgetful「今では物忘れがひどい」

問7 ア.「ロバートソンは大学の学長になるという夢を実現させるのに成功した」第2・3段落第1・2文の内容に一致。

イ.「ロバートソンは早めに辞職したいという夢を持っていたが，彼の夢は実現した」第2・3段落第1・2文の内容に不一致。

ウ.「ロバートソン・マックウィルキンは重い病気になったために仕事を辞めた」第5～7段落第2文の内容に不一致。

エ.「現実主義者は，ロバートソン・マックウィルキンが無責任で利己的だと言った」第5～7段落第4・5文の内容に不一致。

Advice 物語文

物語文は，論説文とは違って，展開を予測しづらい。したがって，登場人物の関係を正確に押さえ，誰の発話であるかに留意しながら話の流れ—誰が何をし，どのようになったか，どのように思ったのか—を捉えることがポイント。また，同じ登場人物が他の登場人物との関係から，様々な呼び方をされることが多いので，注意することが必要。一方，物語文では受験生になじみのない語いや表現が用いられることもあるが，問題になっていない限り，特に細部にとらわれる必要はない。受験生によっては，登場人物の心理の深読みや感情移入をしてしまい，展開が追えなくなってしまうこともあるので，与えられた英文を素直に読むようにしたい。

要　約

マックウィルキンは，アルツハイマー病になった妻の介護のため，大学の学長職を辞した。彼は結婚の際の約束が何よりも重要であると考え，自分のことを認識できなくなった妻を最後

まで介護しようと決意したのだった。(100字)

構文・語句解説

第1段落

[1]One of the most remarkable stories I know is about a man called Robertson McQuilken. [2]As a young man, he dreamed of becoming the president of Columbia Bible College in Columbia, South Carolina. [3]He adored his father, who had held this position, and he hoped to take his father's place someday.

[1]私の知っている最もすばらしい話の1つはロバートソン・マックウィルキンと呼ばれる男に関するものである。[2]若い頃，彼はサウスカロライナのコロンビアにあるコロンビア・バイブル・カレッジの学長になることを夢見ていた。[3]彼は以前この地位にあった父を敬愛していた。そして自分もいつか父と同じ立場に立ちたいと思っていた。

1 I know は the most remarkable stories を修飾する関係代名詞節。

□ remarkable「注目すべき」

2 As a young man の As は「…のときに，…の頃」という意味。

□ dream of *doing*「…することを夢見る」

3 □ adore「を敬愛する」　□ position「立場，地位」(＝place)　□ someday「いつか」

第2・3段落

[1]Robertson McQuilken's dream came true. [2]One day he did become the president of Columbia Bible College. [3]When he became the president, he was convinced that he was called by God and was worthy of that position.

[4]Dr. McQuilken served as president of that college for a number of years, and he did very well and was respected and loved by many people.

[1]ロバートソン・マックウィルキンの夢は実現した。[2]ある日彼は実際にコロンビア・バイブル・カレッジの学長になったのだ。[3]彼は学長になったとき，自分は神によって命じられたのであり，自分はその地位にふさわしいのだ，と確信した。

[4]マックウィルキン博士は何年もの間その大学の学長として務め，実績を上げ，多くの人に尊敬され愛された。

1 □ come true「実現する」

2 did become の did は動詞強調の助動詞。

4 did very well と was respected ... many people が and で結ばれている。後半の受動態の部分は，respected と loved が and で結ばれている。

□ serve as A「Aとして務める」　□ a number of A「いくつかのA，多くのA」

□ do well「うまくいく，成功する」

第4段落

[1]Then one day this man realized he had a tragedy on his hands. [2]His wife began to show the symptoms of Alzheimer's disease. [3]She became worse in a short time, and in a matter of months she was in a terrible situation. [4]She not only lost her memory of much of their life together, but she was unable to even recognize him. [5]She lost all awareness that he was her husband.

[1]それからある日，この男は悲劇に直面していることに気づいた。[2]妻がアルツハイマー病の兆候を見せ始めたのだ。[3]彼女の症状はすぐに悪化し，わずか数ヶ月のうちに深刻な状況に陥った。[4]彼女は二人で過ごした生活の多くの記憶を失ったばかりでなく，彼のことを認識することさえできなくなった。[5]彼女は彼が自分の夫だという意識を失ったのだ。

1 □ have A on *one's* hands「Aに直面している」

2 □ symptom「兆候」　□ Alzheimer's disease「アルツハイマー病」

3 □ a matter of A「ほんのA，わずかなA」　□ terrible「ひどく悪い」

□ situation「状況」

4 □ not only X but (also) Y「XだけでなくYも」　□ memory「記憶」

5 that 以下は awareness と同格の名詞節。　□ awareness「意識」

第5～7段落

[1]Robertson McQuilken made his decision. [2]He resigned the presidency of the college so he could give full-time care to his wife. [3]Without hesitation, he walked away from his job as an act of love for her.

[4]There were some realists who told him there was no meaning in what he was doing. [5]Anybody could take care of his poor wife, they told him, but not anybody could be president of the college. [6]And after all, she didn't even recognize him when he came in the room to help her.

[7]Then there were some religious people who said he was walking away from what God called him to do. [8]He was letting his personal concern for his wife interfere with his more important social responsibility, they said.

[1]ロバートソン・マックウィルキンは決意した。[2]彼は妻の世話が1日じゅうできるように大学の学長の職を辞めた。[3]ためらいもなく彼は妻への愛の行為として職場を去った。

[4]彼がやろうとしていることには何も意味がないと彼に言う現実主義者もいた。[5]誰にでもかわいそうな彼の妻の世話はできるが，誰もが大学の学長になれるわけではない，と彼らは言った。[6]そしてそもそも彼女は彼が世話をしようと部屋に入っていっても，彼のことさえわからないのだ。

[7]それから彼は神がやるように命じたことから去ろうとしていると言う信心深い人もいた。[8]彼は妻に対する気遣いという私的なことによって，もっと重大な社会的責任が果たせなくなっている，と彼らは言った。

1 □ make *one's* decision「決意する」

2 □ resign「を辞職する」　□ presidency「学長の地位」

□ so (that) S can *do*「Sが…するために」　□ full-time「専従の」

3 □ hesitation「ためらい，躊躇」　□ act「行為」

4 □ realist「現実主義者」　□ there is no meaning in A「Aには意味がない」

5 Anybody could ... の Anybody は肯定文で使われているので「誰でも，どんな人でも」の意。Anybody could ... , they told him, but not ... =They told him (that) anybody could ... , but not ...

□ poor「かわいそうな，哀れな」

6 □ after all「そもそも，何と言っても…だから」

8 □ let O *do*「Oが…するままにしておく」　□ concern「気遣い」　□ responsibility「責任」

第8・9段落

[1]The man's answers were magnificent. [2]To the realists he admitted that his wife didn't know who he was. [3]But that wasn't important, he told them. [4]The really important thing was that he still knew who she was and, furthermore, he let them know that he recognized in her now-forgetful self the same lovely woman he had married those many years ago.

[5]Then he turned to the religious people. [6]His words to them were even more profound: "There is only one thing more important than your job. [7]And that is a promise. [8]And I

promised to be there 'until death do us part.'"

[1]その男の答えはすばらしかった。[2]現実主義者に対しては，彼は妻が彼のことを誰であるかわからないということを認めた。[3]しかし，そんなことは重要ではない，と彼は言った。[4]本当に重要なのは，彼女が誰であるのか自分はまだ知っているということなのだ。そのうえ，彼は現実主義者たちに，今では物忘れがひどい彼女の中に自分が何年も前に結婚した同じすてきな女性を認められる，とわかってもらった。

[5]それから彼は信心深い人たちの方を向いた。[6]彼らに対する言葉はよりいっそう感銘深いものであった。「仕事より大切なものがたった１つあるのです。[7]そしてそれは約束です。[8]そして私は彼女に，死が二人を分かつまで一緒にいる，と約束したのです」

1 □ magnificent「すばらしい」

2 □ admit that節「…だと認める」

4 that he ... she was は補語となる名詞節。

□ furthermore「そのうえ，さらに」

5 □ turn to A「Aの方を向く」

6 □ even＋比較級「さらに…，いっそう…」　□ profound「感銘深い」

7 □ promise「約束(する)」

16 週休二日制の始まり

解答

問1　ウ. loved

問2　ウ

問3　労働者は月曜日の仕事を休んで，競馬，クリケットの試合，公共の庭園，美術館，演劇，ダンスホール，社交クラブの集まりに出かけたりもしたから。(68字)

問4　仕事をしない土曜日の午後を与えるような措置は，法律の制定とともに，聖なる月曜日の力を長年の間に徐々に弱めていった，とリードは付け加えている。

問5　a two-day weekend on Saturday and Sunday

問6　ウ

設問解説

問1　空所(1)を含む第1段落第2文は「実際，その日は，もともと月にちなんで名付けられたのだが，かつてはイングランドとアメリカではとても(　1　)ので，『聖なる月曜日』と呼ばれていた」という意味。第1文で「なぜ月曜日が以前はあんなに人気があったのか」と述べられていることから，空所(1)には「人気がある」に近い意味の表現が入ることがわかるが，選択肢の中では，そのような意味を持つのはウの loved「愛される」だけである。したがって，正解はウ。なお，月曜日は「人気」の対象ではあったが，「尊重」の対象ではなかったので，エは不可。

ア.「無視された」イ.「嫌われた」ウ.「愛された」エ.「尊重された」

問2　下線部(2)は「労働者は日曜日だけ仕事が休みだったが，それは教会に行くためであった」という意味。下線部(2)を含む段落の第3文以降に「日曜日が週に唯一の『公認の』休息日であったけれども，多くの労働者たちは日曜日に酒を飲んで二日酔いになり，それから回復しようとしたり，単にくつろいだりするために，月曜日を休むようになった」とあるので，日曜日だけでは休みが足らなかったことがわかる。したがって，正解はウ。

ア.「労働者だけが毎週日曜日に教会に行った」

イ.「労働者は毎週日曜日に教会に行きたいと思った」

ウ.「労働者たちには休息のための時間がほとんどなかった」
エ.「労働者は特別な休日を楽しみにしていた」

問3 下線部(3)は「その日は単に，二日酔いや給料を飲み代に使ってしまうだけの日ではなかった」という意味。「その日」つまり「聖なる月曜日」には他にもすることがあったことがわかる。下線部に続く第3段落第3文に具体的な内容が述べられている。

□ not just ...「ただ…だけではない」　□ involve「に関わる，を伴う」
□ drink A away「A(お金・時間)を酒に費やす」　□ wage「賃金，給料」

問4 adds の目的語となる that 節内は，measures like allowing free Saturday afternoons, ...(S) weakened(V) Saint Monday's dominance(O) という構造になっている。

□ add that 節「…ということを付け加える，付言する」　□ measures「措置」
□ A like B「(たとえば) BのようなA」(＝A such as B)　□ allow「を与える」
□ free「仕事をしなくてよい，暇な」　□ along with A「Aと共に」
□ legislation「法律の制定」　□ gradually「徐々に，ゆっくりと」
□ weaken「を弱める」　□ dominance「(支配する)力，優越」
□ over the years「何年もの間に，長年にわたって」

問5 下線部(5)を含む文は「しかし，この方式は大恐慌まで完全には広まらなかった」という意味。したがって「この方式」は大恐慌以前に導入された方式であることがわかる。直前の第6段落第2文に「1908年にニューイングランドの紡績工場が土曜日と日曜日の週末2日の休みを確立」したとあることから，a two-day weekend on Saturday and Sunday を指すことがわかる。

問6 ア.「労働者が休むことが許されていた唯一の日は教会の休日だったので，皆が聖なる月曜日に賛意を表した」第2段落第2文と第5段落第1文の内容に不一致。
イ.「聖なる月曜日は労働者が教会に行くことを奨励したので，雇用者は聖なる月曜日の習慣が好きではなかった」第5段落第1・2文の内容に不一致。
ウ.「イングランドに聖なる月曜日の慣習があったことが，ある工場経営者が事業をスコットランドに移転させた1つの理由であった」第5段落第3文の内容に一致。
エ.「イングランドには，大恐慌以来，聖なる月曜日の慣習を続けている人がいる」第6段落第4・5文の内容に不一致。

Advice 論説文　主題ー展開型①

論説文では，文章の初めの方で主題が提示され，その主題をめぐって論が展開していくことが多い。したがって，最初の１～２段落は，何が主題であるかを探りながら丁寧に読む必要がある。本問では，第１段落で「以前は人気のあった月曜日が，今日では不人気になってしまったのはなぜだろうか」と述べた後，第２段落以後で，段落ごとにその理由や歴史を述べている。

要約

18，19世紀のイングランドとアメリカでは，日曜日しか休日がなかったので，月曜日を休む人が多く，「聖なる月曜日」と呼ばれていたが，大恐慌以降は週末に２日休む習慣が世界中に広まっている。(90字)

構文・語句解説

第１段落

[1]Here's everything you need to know about why Monday used to be so popular and what's made it so unpopular today. [2]In fact, the day — originally named after the moon — was once loved so much in England and the US that it was called "Saint Monday."

[1]これから書くのは，なぜ月曜日が以前はあんなに人気があったのか，そして今日では月曜日をこんなにも不人気にしてしまったのは何なのかについて知っておく必要のあることのすべてである。[2]実際，その日は，もともと月にちなんで名付けられたのだが，かつてはイングランドとアメリカではとても愛されていたので，「聖なる月曜日」と呼ばれていたのだ。

1 □ need to *do*「…する必要がある」

you need 以下は everything を修飾する関係代名詞節。Here's A は「これがＡである」という意味で，この後に書くことを示している。

□ used to be ...「かつては…であった」　□ popular「人気のある，評判のよい」

□ make O C「ＯをＣにする」　□ unpopular「不人気の，評判の悪い」

2 文全体は so ... that ～ 構文になっている。ダッシュ内の originally named after the moon は分詞構文で，the day の補足説明をしている。

□ in fact「実際，実は」　□ originally「もともと，元来」

□ name A after B「Ｂの名をとってＡに名前を付ける」　□ call O C「ＯをＣと呼ぶ」

□ Saint Monday「聖なる月曜日」

第２段落

[1]Back in the 18th and 19th centuries, the six-day workweek was standard in Britain and

America. [2]Workers only had Sundays off to go to church, along with special holidays like Christmas and New Year that were scattered throughout the calendar. [3]Even though Sunday was the only *official* weekly day of rest, many people still failed to show up on Monday. [4]Many workers would stay home to recover from hangovers after a drunken end to the workweek or just relax and devote some time to leisure. [5]Thus, the phrase "keeping Saint Monday" was born. [6]The habit caught on. [7]According to the writer Witold Rybczynski, it became official practice for workers to take Monday off after a Friday or Saturday payday.

[1]18世紀や19世紀にさかのぼると，週６日労働がイギリスとアメリカでは標準であった。[2]カレンダーのあちこちに散らばっているクリスマスや新年などの特別な休日の他には，労働者が教会に行くために仕事を休むのは日曜日だけだった。[3]日曜日が週に唯一の「公認の」休息日であったけれども，それでも多くの人々は月曜日に出勤しなかった。[4]働いた週を酔っ払って終えた後の二日酔いから回復するために家にいたり，ただくつろいで娯楽にいくらかの時間を充てたりする労働者が多かったのだ。[5]こうして，「聖なる月曜日を続ける」というフレーズが生まれた。[6]この習慣は広く受け入れられた。[7]著述家のヴィトルト・リプチンスキーによれば，金曜日か土曜日の給料日の後に労働者が月曜日を休みにするのが公認の習慣となった。

1 □ workweek「週の労働日数，労働時間」　□ standard「標準的な，普通の」

2 to go to church は目的を表す副詞用法の不定詞句。that were 以下は special holidays を修飾する関係代名詞節。

□ have A off「A（日にちや期間など）を休む」（＝take A off）

□ scatter「をばらまく，あちこちに置く」　□ throughout A「Aの至るところに」

3 □ even though S V ...「…だけれども，たとえ…でも」　□ the only A「唯一のA」

□ official「公認の，正式な」　□ weekly「毎週の」　□ day of rest「休息日」

□ still「それでもなお，それにもかかわらず」　□ fail to *do*「…しない，…できない」

□ show up「姿を現す」

4 or は stay home ... the workweek と just relax ... to leisure の２つの動詞句を結んでいる。and は relax と devote some time to leisure を結んでいる。to recover ... the workweek は目的を表す副詞用法の不定詞句。a drunken end to the workweek は「働いた週を酔っ払って終わること」という意味。

□ would *do*「以前はよく…したものだ」　□ recover from A「Aから回復する」

□ relax「くつろぐ，リラックスする」　□ devote A to B「A（時間）をBに充てる」

□ leisure「余暇，娯楽」

5 □ thus「こうして／したがって」

6 □ habit「(個人の)習慣，癖」　□ catch on「広く行き渡る，人気が出る」

7 it は形式主語で，for workers ... Saturday payday が真主語。

□ according to A「Aによれば」　□ practice「習慣，慣例」　□ payday「給料日」

第3段落

[1]Saint Mondays acquired a somewhat bad reputation for being all about getting drunk, boxing, and blood sports. [2]However, the day didn't *just* involve hangovers or drinking away wages. [3]People would use their day off to visit horse races, cricket matches, public gardens, museums, theater productions, dance halls, and social club meetings.

[1]聖なる月曜日は，酔っ払うことやボクシングや流血を伴うスポーツだけのためにあるということで，いくぶん悪い評判が立った。[2]ところが，その日は単に，二日酔いや給料を飲み代に使ってしまうだけの日ではなかった。[3]人々はその休日を利用して，競馬場，クリケットの試合，公共の庭園，美術館，演劇，ダンスホール，そして社交クラブの集まりを訪れていたのだ。

1 □ acquire「を獲得する，得る」　□ somewhat「やや，いくぶん」

□ be all about A「Aが最も大切である，要するにAである」　□ reputation「評判」

□ get drunk「酔っ払う」　□ boxing「ボクシング」

2 □ however「しかし，ところが」

3 to visit 以下は目的を表す副詞用法の不定詞句。和訳では「結果」のように訳している。and は horse races, cricket matches, public gardens, museums, theater productions, dance halls, social club meetings の7つの名詞句を結んでいる。

□ horse race「競馬」　□ cricket match「クリケットの試合」

□ museum「美術館／博物館」　□ theater production「演劇，舞台作品」

□ social club「社交クラブ」

第4段落

[1]Saint Monday allowed the working class valuable leisure time. [2]In his paper "The Lower Classes and Politics 1800-1850," Michael Richards argues that the tradition gave workers the opportunity to "establish a degree of independence in relation to their employer." [3]In his paper, "The Decline of Saint Monday," Douglas A. Reid refers to an 1851 London writer, who noted that the public gardens "were literally filled with well-dressed, happy and well-behaved working-class people. [4]All appeared to greatly enjoy the

glories of nature.” [5]So Saint Monday wasn’t all about getting drunk.

[1]聖なる月曜日は，労働者階級に貴重な余暇の時間を与えてくれた。[2]『下層階級と政治1800年から1850年まで』という論文の中で，マイケル・リチャーズは，その伝統が労働者に「雇用者との関係におけるある程度の自立を確立する」機会を与えた，と論じている。[3]『聖なる月曜日の衰退』という論文の中で，ダグラス・A・リードは，公共の庭園は「身なりがよく楽しげで行儀のよい労働者階級の人々で文字通り埋め尽くされていた。[4]全員が自然の美しさを大いに楽しんでいるようだった」と述べた1851年のロンドンの著述家に言及している。[5]だから，聖なる月曜日は，酔っ払うことがすべてではなかったのだ。

1 □ allow O_1 O_2「O_1に O_2を与える」　□ working class「労働者階級」

□ valuable「貴重な，価値のある」　□ leisure time「余暇(の時間)」

2 第2文の the tradition は Saint Monday を指す。

□ paper「論文」　□ lower class「下層階級」　□ politics「政治」

□ argue that 節「…だと論じる，主張する」　□ opportunity to *do*「…する機会」

□ establish「を確立する」　□ a degree of A「ある程度のA」

□ independence「自立，独立」　□ in relation to A「Aとの関係において」

□ employer「雇用者」

3 who 以下は an 1851 London writer を補足説明する非制限用法の関係代名詞節。and は well-dressed, happy, well-behaved の3つの形容詞を結んでいる。

□ decline「衰退，凋落」　□ refer to A「Aに言及する，Aについて語る」

□ note that 節「…だと述べる／…ということに注目する」

□ be filled with A「Aでいっぱいである」　□ literally「文字通り，本当に」

□ well-dressed「立派な服装をした，身なりのよい」　□ well-behaved「行儀のよい」

4 □ appear to *do*「…するようである，…するように見える」　□ greatly「大いに」

□ glory「美しさ，栄光」

第5段落

[1]Obviously, not everyone loved this custom. [2]Business owners felt that the day off hurt their productivity. [3]According to Reid’s research, one factory owner moved his chemical works from Birmingham to Scotland in 1766, partly due to the custom of Saint Monday in England. [4]As Rybczynski previously noted, in order to stop people from taking time off, shops and factories started closing earlier on Saturdays. [5]Reid adds that measures like allowing free Saturday afternoons, along with legislation, gradually weakened Saint

Monday's dominance over the years.

[1]誰もがこの慣習を好んでいるわけではなかったのは明らかである。[2]会社の経営者は休日には生産性が低下すると思っていた。[3]リードの調査によれば，ある工場経営者が1766年に化学工場をバーミンガムからスコットランドに移転させたが，理由の１つはイングランドの聖なる月曜日の慣習であった。[4]リプチンスキーが前に指摘しているように，人々が休みを取らないようにするために，商店や工場が毎週土曜日には，より早い時刻に営業をやめ始めた。[5]仕事をしない土曜日の午後を与えるような措置は，法律の制定とともに，聖なる月曜日の力を長年の間に徐々に弱めていった，とリードは付け加えている。

1 not everyone ... は「誰もが…するわけではない」という部分否定を表す。

□ obviously「(文修飾で)明らかに」　□ custom「慣習」

2 □ business owner「会社の経営者」　□ hurt「を害する，に悪影響を与える」

□ productivity「生産性」

3 □ research「調査，研究」　□ factory owner「工場経営者」

□ move A from B to C「AをBからCに移転させる」　□ chemical works「化学工場」

□ partly「１つには，ある程度は」　□ due to A「Aのせいで，Aが原因で」

4 □ in order to *do*「…するために」

□ stop A from *doing*「Aが…するのをやめさせる，妨げる」

□ close「(店などが)閉まる，営業を終える」　□ on Saturdays「毎週土曜日に」

第６段落

[1]Our current practice of a 40-hour workweek and two-day weekend has its roots in the Industrial Revolution and the gradual decline of Saint Monday. [2]In 1908, a New England cotton mill established a two-day weekend on Saturday and Sunday, to allow both Jewish and Christian workers to worship on their respective holy days. [3]However, this model didn't fully catch on until the Great Depression. [4]This standard workweek is now widely accepted around the world. [5]And thus, as the first day of the standard workweek, the once merry Monday was forgotten.

[1]週40時間労働で週末に２日休むという私たちの現在の習慣は，産業革命が起きたことと聖なる月曜日が徐々に衰退したことにその起源を持つ。[2]1908年に，ニューイングランドの紡績工場が土曜日と日曜日の週末２日の休みを確立し，ユダヤ教徒とキリスト教徒の両方の労働者がそ

れぞれの聖日に礼拝ができるようになった。[3]しかし，この方式は大恐慌まで完全には広まらなかった。[4]この標準的な1週間の労働時間は，今や世界中で広く受け入れられている。[5]そして，このようにして，標準的な働く週の初日として，かつては楽しかった月曜日が忘れられたのである。

1 1つめの and は a 40-hour workweek と two-day weekend を結んでいる。2つめの and は the Industrial Revolution と the gradual decline of Saint Monday を結んでいる。

□ current「現在の」　□ two-day weekend「2日間の週末」

□ have *one's* roots in A「Aに起源を持つ」

□ the Industrial Revolution「産業革命」　□ gradual「徐々の，ゆっくりとした」

2 to allow 以下は結果を表す副詞用法の不定詞句。

□ New England「(アメリカ東部の)ニューイングランド地方」　□ cotton mill「紡績工場」

□ allow O to *do*「Oが…できるようにする」　□ Jewish「ユダヤ教徒」

□ Christian「キリスト教徒」　□ worship「礼拝に出る，教会に行く」

□ respective「それぞれの」　□ holy day「聖日」

3 □ not fully ...「完全に…するわけではない」

4 □ widely「広く」　□ accept「を受け入れる」　□ around the world「世界中で」

5 □ as A「Aとして」　□ once「かつては」　□ merry「楽しい」

17 脳の拡大

解　答

問1　生命の歴史の中で，それほど急速な発達を遂げたと知られている器官は他にない。

問2　エ. A change of climate that set in about two million years ago

問3　非常に多くの水が氷という形で陸地に閉じ込められたため，地球の海洋の水位は300フィート下がった。

問4　アフリカからアラビアを越え，北に向かい，アジアへと東に，ヨーロッパへと西に，移動したこと。(45字)

問5　such inventive and imaginative acts could human beings survive

問6　エ

設問解説

問1　否定語＋as＋原級＋as ...「…ほど～なものはない」という表現の as ... が省略されている。as the brain と補うことができる。訳出上は「それほど～なものはない」でよい。is known to have grown は述語動詞 is が現在形なのに対して，不定詞句の内容が過去から現在に至る時間に及ぶことなので完了形になっている。

□ organ「器官」　□ be known to *do*「…すると知られている」

問2　空所(2)を含む文は，直前の文で提示された問い「どのような圧力が人間の脳の爆発的な発達を生み出したのだろう」に対する答えとなる可能性があるものを述べた文である。第2段落第3文以降で「同時期が氷河時代であった」ことが述べられ，第4～7段落で「氷河時代を生き延びるために人間は創意工夫しなければならなかった」ということが述べられている。したがって，「気候」に関するものを選ぶ。

ア.「最初の氷河期に定着した衣服の着用という習慣」

イ.「人間が恐竜と戦わなければならなかったという事実」

ウ.「言語の発明と道具の使用」

エ.「およそ200万年前に始まった気候の変化」

問3　so ... that～「とても…なので～，～するほど…」の構文である。このように so と that 以下が離れている場合は，見落としがちなので注意が必要。なお，

by three hundred feet の by は程度・差を表し「…だけ」という意味。

□ lock A up「Aを閉じ込める」　□ in the form of A「Aという形で」

問4 第3・4段落第3文に The movements of humans とあり，これを具体的に述べたのが第6文である。

問5 Only by が文頭にきているため，倒置が起きる。また，第6段落第1文に「そのような困難な時に，工夫と創意に富んでいることはとても価値があった」とあり，第4文には「どの世代でも，力と勇気と創造性を備えた者が氷河時代を生き延びる可能性が高かった」とあることから，「そのような創意に富み想像力あふれる行為によってはじめて人間は寒い気候を生き延びることができた」という意味の英文が求められている。

□ inventive「創意に富む」　□ imaginative「想像力あふれる」　□ act「行為」

□ survive「(を)生き延びる」

問6 ア.「人間の脳の発達の割合はおよそ50万年前にピークを迎えた」第1段落第3文の内容に一致。

イ.「200万年前に氷河時代が始まった後，北方に広大な領域の氷ができるのにおよそ100万年かかった」第2段落第4文の内容に一致。

ウ.「工夫や創意にそれほど富んでいないものは，氷河時代を生き延びることはできなかった」第6段落第4文の内容に一致。

エ.「氷河時代の人間は1億年前の小型哺乳動物と共通点は何もなかった」第7段落第2・3文の内容と不一致。

Advice 論説文　主題ー展開型②

論説文中の疑問文には注意する必要がある。疑問文という形で筆者が読み手に問題を投げかけ，これが以下の内容の主題になることが多いからである。本問では，第2段落第1文の疑問文で提示された「どのような圧力が人間の脳の発達を生み出したのか」という問題に対して，「寒冷化という要因の可能性」が第2段落で述べられ，さらに第3段落第2文の疑問文で提示された「脳の拡大と寒冷化が同時期であったのは意味のあることなのか，偶然なのか」という問題をめぐって，そこから後ろでは論が展開している。

要　約

およそ100万年前から人間の脳が急速に発達したのは，同時期の氷河時代を生き延びるために人間は創意工夫しなければならなかったからである。(65字)

構文・語句解説

第1段落

[1]Starting about one million years ago, there was an increase in the growth of the human brain. [2]It expanded at first at the rate of one cubic inch every hundred thousand years; then the growth rate doubled; it doubled again; and finally it doubled once more. [3]Five hundred thousand years ago the rate of growth hit its peak. [4]At that time the brain was expanding at a rate of ten cubic inches every hundred thousand years. [5]No other organ in the history of life is known to have grown as fast.

[1]およそ100万年前から，人間の脳の発達が増大し始めた。[2]当初10万年に１立方インチの割合で拡大していたものが，発達の割合は２倍になり，再び２倍になり，さらにもう一度２倍になった。[3]50万年前には，発達の割合はピークを迎えた。[4]当時，脳は10万年に10立方インチの割合で拡大していた。[5]生命の歴史の中で，それほど急速な発達を遂げたと知られている器官は他にない。

1 Starting about one million years ago は分詞構文。

2 □ expand「拡大する」　□ at first「最初のうちは」　□ at the rate of A「Aの割合で」
□ every＋数詞＋複数名詞「…毎に」　□ double「２倍になる」

3 □ hit a peak「ピークを迎える，頂点に達する」

第2段落

[1]What pressures generated the explosive growth of the human brain? [2]A change of climate that set in about two million years ago may supply part of the answer. [3]At that time the world began to enter into a great Ice Age, the first on the planet in hundreds of millions of years. [4]The trend toward colder weather set in slowly at first, but after a million years areas of ice began to form in the north. [5]They thickened into glaciers as more snow fell, and then the glaciers joined together into great sheets of ice, as much as two miles thick. [6]When the ice sheets reached their maximum extent, they covered two-thirds of the North American continent, all of Britain and a large part of Europe. [7]Many mountain ranges were buried entirely. [8]So much water was locked up on the land in the form of ice that the level of the earth's oceans dropped by three hundred feet.

[1]どのような圧力が人間の脳の爆発的な発達を生み出したのだろう。[2]およそ200万年前に始ま

った気候の変化がその答えの一部になるかもしれない。³その頃世界は，数億年で初めて地球で起きた大氷河時代に入ろうとしていた。⁴寒冷化の傾向は，最初はゆっくりと始まったが，100万年後には氷の地域が北方で形成され始めた。⁵さらに雪が降るにつれて，氷の地域が厚くなって氷河となり，氷河はつながって，２マイルもの厚さのある巨大な氷床となった。⁶氷床が最大限に達したとき，北米大陸の３分の２，イギリス全土，ヨーロッパの大部分を覆っていた。⁷多くの山脈は完全に埋没した。⁸非常に多くの水が氷という形で陸地に閉じ込められたため，地球の海洋の水位は300フィート下がった。

1 □ pressure「圧力」　□ generate「を生み出す」　□ explosive「爆発的な」

2 □ supply「を与える」　3 □ Ice Age「氷河時代」

3 □ hundreds of millions of A「数億のA」　4 □ form「形を成す」

5 as much as two miles thick は great sheets of ice を修飾。as much as は two miles thick を強調している。

□ thicken into A「厚くなってAになる」　□ glacier「氷河」

□ join together into A「つながってAになる」　□ sheet of ice「氷床」

6 □ maximum「最大の」　□ extent「程度，限度」　□ two-thirds「３分の２」

7 □ mountain range「山脈」　□ bury「を埋める」　□ entirely「完全に」

第３・４段落

[1]These events occurred precisely at the same time as the period of most rapid expansion of the human brain. [2]Is this significant, or is it accidental?

[3]The movements of humans in the last million years provide a clue to the answer. [4]At the beginning of the Ice Age, humans lived near the equator, where the climate was mild and pleasant. [5]Later they moved northward. [6]From their birthplace in Africa they moved up across Arabia and then turned to the north and west into Europe, as well as eastward into Asia.

¹これらの現象は人間の脳の最も急速な拡大の時期とまったく同じ時期に起きたのである。²このことは意味のあることなのであろうか，あるいは偶然なのだろうか？

³過去100万年間の人類の移動が答えの手がかりを与えてくれる。⁴氷河時代の最初の頃，人類は気候が温暖で快適な赤道付近で暮らしていた。⁵その後，人類は北に向かって移動した。⁶アフリカの人類発祥の地から，アラビアを横断して，北に向かい，ヨーロッパへと西に，そしてアジアへと東にも移動した。

1 □ precisely「まさに，正確に」　□ expansion「拡大」

2 □ significant「意味のある」　□ accidental「偶然の」

3 □ provide「を与える」　□ clue to A「Aの手がかり」

4 □ equator「赤道」　5 □ northward「北へ」

6 west into Europe, as well as eastward into Asia において X as well as Y「XもYも／Yだけでなく Xも」の X には west into Europe が Y には eastward into Asia がきている。

□ Arabia「アラビア半島」　□ eastward「東へ」

第5段落

[1]When these early movements took place, the ice still only covered the lands in the far north; but eight hundred thousand years ago, the ice moved southward until it covered large parts of Europe and Asia. [2]Then, for the first time, humans encountered the bone-chilling, freezing winds from the cakes of ice in the north. [3]The climate in southern Europe had a Siberian coldness then, and summers were nearly as cold as European winters are today.

[1]このような初期の移動が行われたとき，氷はまだ最北部の地を覆っていただけだった。しかし，80万年前に，ヨーロッパとアジアの大部分を覆うまで氷は南下した。[2]そのとき人類は初めて，北の氷のかたまりから吹く骨までしみるような，凍てつく風を知った。[3]当時南ヨーロッパの気候にはシベリアの寒さがあり，夏は今日のヨーロッパの冬とほぼ同じくらい寒かった。

1 □ take place「行われる，起きる」　□ cover「を覆う」　□ southward「南へ」

2 □ for the first time「初めて」　□ encounter「と遭遇する」

□ bone-chilling「骨までしみるような」　□ freezing「凍てつく」　□ cake「かたまり」

3 □ Siberian「シベリアの」

第6段落

[1]In those difficult times, resourcefulness and inventiveness must have been of great value. [2]Which individual first thought of stripping the fur from dead animals to wrap around his body? [3]Only by such inventive and imaginative acts could human beings survive a cold climate. [4]In every generation, the individuals with strength, courage, and creativity were the ones more likely to survive the Ice Age; those who were less resourceful fell victim to the climate and their numbers were reduced.

[1]そのような困難なときに，工夫と創意に富んでいることはとても価値があったに違いない。[2]身体をくるむために死んだ動物から毛皮を剥ぎ取ることを最初に思いついたのは誰だったのだろうか？[3]そのような創意に富み想像力あふれる行為によって初めて人間は寒い気候を生き延びることができた。[4]どの世代でも，力と勇気と創造性を備えた者が氷河時代を生き延びる可能性が高かった者であり，工夫の才能が劣るものは気候の犠牲となり，そうした者の数は減ったのである。

1 □ resourcefulness「工夫に富んでいること」　□ inventiveness「発明の才能」
□ must have *done*「…だったに違いない」　□ of value「価値のある」
2 □ strip A from B「BからAを剥ぎ取る」　□ fur「毛皮」　□ wrap around A「Aをくるむ」
4 the ones more likely to survive the Ice Age の more likely 以下は the ones を修飾。ones は individuals の代用。　□ creativity「創造性」
□ those who ...「…する人々」　□ fall victim to A「Aの犠牲となる」　□ reduce「を減らす」

第7段落

[1]The Ice Age winter was the greatest challenge that humans had ever faced. [2]They were naked and defenseless against the cold, as some little mammals had been defenseless against the dinosaurs one hundred million years before. [3]Facing the pressures of a hostile world, both those mammals and humans were forced to live by their wits; and both became, in their time, the most intelligent animals of the day.

[1]氷河時代の冬は人類がそれまでに直面した中で最大の難題であった。[2]その1億年前に小型哺乳動物が恐竜に対して無防備であったのと同様に，人類も衣服をまとわず寒さに対して無防備であった。[3]敵意にみちた世界からの圧力に直面して，そうした哺乳動物と人類は，知恵を働かせて生きていくことを余儀なくされた。そして，両者はそれぞれの時代に，最も知能の高い動物となったのである。

1 □ challenge「難題」　□ face「に直面する」
2 □ naked「裸の」　□ defenseless against A「Aに対して無防備の」　□ mammal「哺乳動物」
□ dinosaur「恐竜」
3 Facing the pressures of a hostile world は分詞構文。
□ hostile「敵意にみちた，敵意のある」　□ force O to *do*「Oに…することを強いる」
□ live by *one's* wits「知恵を働かせて生きていく」　□ intelligent「知能の高い」

18 ホッキョクグマ

解答

問1　ホッキョクグマが氷の接岸を待っている。

問2　クマは，固まって巨大な広がりを生み出す浮氷の上でほとんどいつも生活をするが，その巨大な広がりはクマが泳いで渡る小さな開水域で隔てられている。

問3　クマが寒さの中を生き延びるために使う分厚い脂肪の層に PCB がたまり，その後 PCB がクマの内分泌系に影響を与えて性転換を引き起こすことがある。

問4　ウ．dark

問5　エ

問6　ウ

設問解説

問1　下線部(1)の waiting は前の文の後半にある leaving dozens of underweight and hungry bears roaming on the beaches waiting for its return を受けると考えられるので，wait の主語は dozens of underweight and hungry bears「何十頭ものやせて腹をすかせたクマ」であることがわかる。また its return は前の文の主語となっている the return of the ice の言い換えであり，「氷が戻ってくること」すなわち「浮氷が陸地に再び接岸すること」を指す。以上を簡潔にまとめればよい。

問2　The bears(S) live(V) almost entirely on floating ice(副詞句) がこの文の基本構造。that packs ... swim across は floating ice を修飾する関係代名詞節。separated by ... open water は expanses を修飾する過去分詞句であり，that they swim across は open water を修飾する関係代名詞節。separated 以下の直訳は「クマが泳いで渡る小さな開水域によって隔てられた」であるが，後置修飾がいくつも続く形なので，解答例のように途中で一度切った方が意味が伝わりやすい。なお，packs together to create vast expanses の to create vast expanses は，文脈から目的ではなく結果を表す不定詞句と判断し，「固まって巨大な広がりを生み出す」と訳出する。

例　The show went on to become a great success.

「公演は続き，大成功をおさめた」

□ almost entirely「ほぼ完全に」　□ floating ice「浮氷」

□ pack together「〈雪・氷が〉(吹き寄せられて)固まる」　□ vast「巨大な」

□ expanse「広がり，広々とした場所」　□ separate「を隔てる，分ける」

□ open water「開水域」海水の凍っていない部分のこと。

問3 全体の文構造は The huge ... the cold(S) collect(V) PCBs(O) である。used by bears to survive in the cold の過去分詞句が The huge layers of fat を修飾している。また，which 以下は PCBs を補足説明する非制限用法の関係代名詞節であり，その節内で affect their hormonal systems と can cause sex changes の2つの動詞句が and で結ばれている。

□ huge「巨大な」　□ layer「層」　□ fat「脂肪」　□ survive「生き延びる」

□ in the cold「寒さの中で」

□ PCB「ポリ塩化ビフェニル」(＝polychlorinated biphenyl) 催奇性，発癌(はつがん)性が疑われている。

□ affect「に影響を与える」　□ cause「を引き起こす」　□ sex change「性転換」

問4 英文全体の内容から，ホッキョクグマの将来は悲観的なものであることは明らか。したがって，正解はウ。

ア.「明るい」　イ.「バラ色の」　ウ.「暗い」　エ.「前途有望な」

問5 アは第5段落，イは第4段落第1・2文，ウは第4段落第3・4文にそれぞれ述べられているが，エは本文中に該当する記述がない。

問6 ア. 第5段落第5文に Wadhams の見解として述べられている。

イ. 第2段落第1文に Wadhams の見解として述べられている。

ウ. 第3段落第2文の Schliebe の見解と不一致。

エ. 第2段落第3文に Schliebe の見解として述べられている。

Advice 論説文　主題ー展開型③

新聞や雑誌の記事では，最初の段落で記事全体の概要が述べられ，以下の段落で補足的内容や，より詳しい説明が行われることが多い。したがって，最初の段落をしっかりと把握すれば，記事全体の大まかな内容がつかめることになる。本問では，最初に見出しがあることや，本文中に固有名詞が多いことなどから，記事文であると推測できる。

要約

北極地方の温暖化により氷が縮小したことが，狩猟や汚染により個体数を減らしていたホッキョクグマの生存に脅威となっている。一方，北極海が1年中航海できる可能性が出てきている。(85字)

▶▶▶ 構文・語句解説 ◀◀◀

第１段落

Can the Polar Bear Survive?

[1]The rapid shrinking of the Arctic ice cap is threatening the world's polar bear population, scientists have warned. [2]Studies suggest the decline in the thickness and extent of the ice cap is causing the deaths of hundreds of bears a year. [3]The total polar bear population is estimated at only 25,000. [4]Many spend long periods trapped on land, where they find it hard to feed, rather than on ice, while young bears are dying in dens that melt and collapse.

ホッキョクグマは生き残れるか？

[1]北極の氷原の急速な縮小が世界のホッキョクグマの数を脅かしている，と科学者は警告してきた。[2]様々な調査が示すところによると，氷原の厚さと広さの減少が１年に何百頭ものクマの死を引き起こしているのである。[3]ホッキョクグマの総数はわずか25,000頭と推定されている。[4]その多くが氷の上ではなく，エサを探すのが困難な陸地に長期間閉じ込められて過ごすが，一方で幼いクマは溶けて崩れる巣穴の中で死んでいっている。

1 The rapid ... bear population, scientists have warned. = Scientists have warned that the rapid ... bear population.

□ shrinking「縮小，縮み」　□ Arctic「北極(の)，北極地方(の)」
□ ice cap「〈常に氷と雪で覆われた〉氷原／〈惑星の極などの〉氷冠」
□ threaten「を脅かす」　□ polar bear「ホッキョクグマ」polar は「極地の」の意味。
□ population「〈動物の〉個体数／人口」　□ warn「を警告する」

2 □ study「調査，研究」　□ suggest (that) 節「…ということを示唆する」
□ decline in A「Aの減少，低下」　□ thickness「厚さ」　□ extent「範囲，広さ」
□ hundreds of A「何百ものA」　□ a year「１年につき」

3 □ total「全体の，合計の」
□ estimate A at B「A〈数・量など〉をBだと推定する，見積もる」

4 Many = Many polar bears
where they ... to feed は land を補足説明する関係副詞節。X rather than Y「YというよりむしろX」の X に on land，Y に on ice がきている。
□ spend A *done*「A〈時間・期間〉を…されて過ごす」　□ trap「〈人・動物〉を閉じ込める」
□ on land「陸地に」　□ feed「〈動物が〉物を食べる」　□ while S V ...「一方では…」
□ melt「溶ける」　□ collapse「崩れる，崩壊する」

第２段落

[1]Research by Dr. Peter Wadhams shows that the summer ice now averages just 9 feet in thickness compared with 16 feet 20 years ago. [2]He predicts that all the polar ice will disappear during the summer months by about 2080. [3]However, the bears will suffer disastrous declines long before then. [4]Around Hudson Bay in Canada the increasing warmth has forced bears onto land when the ice melts from July to October. [5]In recent years, however, the return of the ice has been delayed by up to a month—leaving dozens of underweight and hungry bears roaming on the beaches waiting for its return. [6]The animals cannot easily find food on land, so every day spent waiting means that they consume more fat reserves.

[1]ピーター・ワダムズ博士による研究は，現在の夏の氷の平均的な厚さは，20年前の16フィートに比べて，９フィートしかないことを示している。[2]2080年頃までに極地の氷はすべて夏の月の間は消えてしまう，と彼は予想している。[3]ところが，クマの数はそのずっと前に壊滅的に減少することになるだろう。[4]カナダのハドソン湾の辺りでは，氷が溶ける７月から10月までは，ますます暖かくなっているためクマは陸に上がることを強いられている。[5]ところが，近年になって，氷が戻ってくるのが１ヶ月も遅くなっていて，何十頭ものやせて腹をすかせたクマが氷が戻るのを待ちながら海岸をさまよっている。[6]この動物たちは陸では簡単に食べ物を探すことができないので，待って過ごす１日ごとに，よけいに脂肪の蓄えを消費することになる。

1 □ research「研究，調査」　□ average「〈平均して〉になる」

□ feet<foot「〈長さの単位〉フィート」の複数形。１フィートは約30cm。

□ compared with A「Aと比べて」

2 □ predict that 節「…だと予測する，予言する」

3 □ suffer「〈被害・影響など〉を受ける，被る」　□ disastrous「壊滅的な，悲惨な」

□ long before A「Aのずっと前に」

4 □ Hudson Bay「ハドソン湾」カナダ北東部の湾。

□ force A onto land「Aを陸地へ追い出す」

5 leaving 以下は分詞構文。また，waiting 以下は roaming に対する付帯状況を表す分詞構文。

□ recent「最近の」　□ return「戻ること」　□ delay「を遅らせる」

□ by A「Aだけ，Aの分」差を表す。　□ up to A「〈最高〉Aまで」

□ leave O *doing*「Oを…しているままに放っておく」　□ dozens of A「何十ものA」

□ underweight「重量不足の，やせた」　□ roam「ぶらつく，放浪する」

6 spent waiting は every day を修飾する過去分詞句。

□ consume「を消費する」　□ fat reserves「脂肪の蓄え」

第3段落

[1]Scott Schliebe said huge changes in the biology of the Arctic were apparent. [2]"The pack ice is already diminishing every summer and without pack ice I cannot see how the bears would survive. [3]They are not adapted for living on land," he said. [4]The bears live almost entirely on floating ice that packs together to create vast expanses separated by small areas of open water that they swim across. [5]They are superbly adapted for survival in the frozen north, eating mainly seals. [6]They range across a huge area of ice controlled by Russia, America, Canada, Greenland, and Norway. [7]Adult males reach weights of 1,500 pounds and are among the fiercest and most dangerous of animals.

[1]スコット・シュリーベは，北極の生態における大きな変化は明らかである，と述べた。[2]「パックアイスはすでに夏ごとに減りつつあり，パックアイスがなければクマがどうやって生き残っていくのかわかりません。[3]クマは地上で生きることには適していないのです」と彼は言った。[4]クマは，固まって巨大な広がりを生み出す浮氷の上でほとんどいつも生活をするが，その巨大な広がりはクマが泳いで渡る小さな開水域で隔てられている。[5]クマは北の凍った地方で，主にアザラシを食べながら生き延びていくことに見事に適応している。[6]クマはロシア，アメリカ，カナダ，グリーンランド，そしてノルウェーによって管理されている巨大な氷原のあちこちに生息している。[7]成長したオスは体重が1,500ポンドにも達し，最もどう猛で危険な動物のうちに数えられる。

1 □ biology「生態／生物学」　□ be apparent「明らかである」

2 without pack ice は how the bears would survive という仮定法の帰結節に対する条件を表す前置詞句。

□ diminish「小さくなる，縮小する」　□ see how S V ...「どのように…するのかわかる」

3 □ be adapted for A「Aに適している」

5 eating mainly seals は分詞構文。

□ superbly「すばらしく，見事に」　□ survival「生存，生き延びること」

□ frozen「凍った」　□ mainly「主に，主として」

6 □ range「〈動植物が〉分布する，生息する」　□ across A「Aのいたる所に」

7 □ adult「〈動植物が〉成長した，成熟した」　□ male「オス」　□ weight「体重」

□ pound「〈重さの単位〉ポンド」 1ポンドは約0. 45kg。　□ be among A「Aの1つである」

□ fierce「どう猛な」

第4段落

[1]Bears have long been hunted by humans for meat and fur. [2]The numbers to be destroyed are now strictly controlled by international agreements but hundreds are still killed each year. [3]Humans also present another threat to bears — through pollution of the sea with poisonous chemicals called PCBs, which accumulate in fat. [4]The huge layers of fat used by bears to survive in the cold collect PCBs, which then affect their hormonal systems and can cause sex changes.

[1]クマは肉と毛皮のために，長い間，人間による狩りの対象となってきた。[2]狩られる数は国際協定によって今では厳しく規制されているが，今でも毎年何百頭も殺されている。[3]人間はまた，脂肪に蓄積する PCB と呼ばれる毒性のある化学物質で海を汚染することを通じて，クマに別の脅威も与えている。[4]クマが寒さの中を生き延びるために使う分厚い脂肪の層に PCB がたまり，その後 PCB がクマの内分泌系に影響を与えて性転換を引き起こすことがある。

1 □ long「長い間」　□ hunt「を狩る，狩猟する」　□ humans「人間」　□ fur「毛皮」

2 The numbers to be destroyed は「(狩猟によって)殺されてもよい数」という意味。

□ be destroyed「〈動物などが〉殺される」kill の婉曲表現。　□ strictly「厳しく」

□ international agreement「国際協定」

3 □ present A to B「A〈困難など〉をBに与える」　□ threat「脅威」

□ pollution of A with B「AをBで汚染すること」　□ poisonous「毒性のある」

□ chemical「化学物質」　□ accumulate「蓄積する，たまる」

第5段落

[1]Scientists say the warming of the Arctic is largely due to rising global temperatures. [2]The direct effect is to melt the ice from above — but the indirect effect is even more destructive. [3]Wadhams' research shows that the Gulf Stream and other currents that carry warm water north have become stronger, warming water beneath the ice cap to melt it from below, too. [4]Another effect of the melting ice will be to open up the shipping routes between Europe, northern Russia and the Far East and to end the annual winter isolation of Siberia. [5]"In the next few years we are going to see the opening up of the Arctic Ocean to year-round traffic," said Wadhams. [6]"Eventually the northwest passage around Canada may open up, too. [7]It will completely alter our trading patterns — but for bears

the future could be dark.”

[1]科学者は，北極地方の温暖化は主に地球の気温の上昇が原因である，と言っている。[2]直接的な影響は，氷が上から溶けることだが，間接的な影響はさらに破壊的である。[3]ワダムズの研究は，暖かい海水を北に運んでくるメキシコ湾流やその他の海流が強くなり，氷原の下の海水を温め，下からもそれを溶かしている，ということを示している。[4]氷が溶けていくことのもう１つの影響は，ヨーロッパ，ロシア北部，そして極東との間の航路が開かれることであり，シベリアが毎年冬に孤立しているのが終わることである。[5]「今後数年の間に，北極海に１年じゅう船の行き来が始まるのを私たちは目にすることになるだろう」とワダムズは言った。[6]「やがては，カナダを回る北西航路も開かれるかもしれない。[7]それは私たちの貿易のパターンを完全に変えることだろう。しかし，クマにとっては，将来は暗いであろう」

1 □ warming「温暖化」　□ largely「主に，主として」　□ be due to A「Aのせいである」
□ global「地球の」

2 □ effect「影響／結果」　□ from above「上から」
□ even＋比較級「さらに…，いっそう…」
□ destructive「破壊的な」

3 warming 以下は連続・結果の分詞構文で，become stronger に対する補足説明となっている。to melt 以下は結果を表す不定詞句。
□ currents「海流」　□ warm「を暖める」　□ beneath A「Aの下に(ある)」
□ from below「下から」

4 □ open A up「A を切り開く」　□ shipping route「航路，海路」
□ the Far East「極東地方」日本や朝鮮半島などアジア大陸の東端の地区。
□ annual「毎年の」　□ isolation「孤立」　□ Siberia「シベリア」

5 □ the Arctic Ocean「北極海」　□ year-round「１年じゅうの」
□ traffic「交通，行き来」ここでは「船で行き来できること」という意味。

6 □ eventually「やがては，最終的に」　□ northwest「北西の」　□ passage「航路，通路」

7 □ completely「完全に」　□ alter「を変える」　□ trading「貿易の」

19 インターネットの悪影響

解　答

問1　以前は本や長い記事に没頭するのは私には簡単だったが，もはやそんなことはまれにしかない。

問2　saves

問3　集中力と思考力が低下すること。

問4　若い人がインターネットの影響で，ページを必ずしも左から右へ，また上から下へと読まずに，飛ばし読みをして，興味のある重要な情報のみを拾うようになっていること。(78字)

問5　ウ．a thing of the past

設問解説

問1　前半の find it easy to get ... は，find O C「OをCだと思う，OがCだとわかる」の O が形式目的語の it，C が easy，to get 以下が真目的語となった形。but 以下には，be the case「あてはまる，実情である」の表現が用いられている。

□used to *do*「以前はよく…したものだ」　□get lost in A「Aに集中する，没頭する」

□article「記事」　□rarely「めったに…ない」

問2　空所(2)を含む文は「私は著述家なので，調べ物をしているときはインターネットのおかげでたくさんの時間を(　2　)」という意味，その後の2文も「コンピュータを便利に使っている」という趣旨になっていることから，空所(2)には「インターネットが大いに時間を省いてくれる」という意味になるように，save を入れる。save は，save O_1 O_2 で「O_1(人)の O_2(時間・お金など)を省く」という意味になる。ただし，主語が the internet なので，三単現の s の付いた saves が正解となる。なお，spare は，spare O_1 O_2 で「O_1(人)の O_2(労力・手間など)を省く」という意味では save と同意になるが，O_2 に「時間」がくると「O_1(人)に O_2(時間)を割く」という意味になるので，本問では不可。

問3　名詞の price には「値段，価格」という意味の他に，「代償，犠牲」という意味があり，at a price で「大きな代償を払って」という意味になる。「大きな代償」とは，同段落第6文の「そして，インターネットがやっているように思えるのは，私の集中力と思考力を低下させることである」に書かれているので，この文の後半をまとめればよい。

問 4 下線部(4)は「インターネットは若者たちが情報を吸収する方法に影響を与えてきている」という意味だが，その影響の具体的な内容は直後の 2 文に書かれているので，この内容をまとめる。

□ affect「に影響を与える」　□ absorb「を吸収する」

問 5 空所(5)を含む第 5 段落最終文の主語 that mind とは，同段落第 1 文で述べられている a 'linear' mind「『直線的な』知性」のことであるが，続く第 2 文で「その知性が変わりつつある」こと，第 3 文で「印刷機が発明されてから 5 世紀にわたり，その知性は芸術，科学，社会の中心であった」ことが述べられている。したがって，「今はその知性が『過去のもの』となっているのかもしれない」とすればよいので，正解はウ。

ア.「著述家にのみ有用な」イ.「かつてないほど重要な」ウ.「過去のもの」
エ.「識字障害の一因」

Advice 論説文　導入－主題－展開型

論説文によっては，導入部分に続いて，主題が中頃の段落で提示されることがある。本問では，第 1 段落で「自分の知性が衰えていく」ことへの不安が述べられた後，第 2 ～ 3 段落で「インターネットを頻繁に利用することが人間の思考力や文章の読み方に与える悪影響」という主題が提示され，それ以降ではこの主題をめぐって論が展開している。問 4 と問 5 は，このような論旨展開を追うことができたかどうかを問う問題である。

要　約

印刷機の発明以来，人間は長い文章を集中して読む能力を持ってきたが，インターネットの普及により，特に若い人たちの間で，飛ばし読みをして重要な情報のみを拾う読み方が広まり，その能力を失いつつある。(96字)

構文・語句解説

第 1 段落

[1]I feel like I'm losing my mind. [2]Over the last few years, I've had an uncomfortable feeling that someone, or something, has been changing the way my brain works. [3]I haven't completely lost my mind, but I can feel it's changing. [4]I feel it most strongly when I'm reading. [5]I used to find it easy to get lost in a book or a long article, but that's rarely the case anymore. [6]Now my concentration starts to drift after a page or two. [7]I read a little bit, then start looking for something else to do. [8]I feel like I'm

always pulling my lazy brain back to the text.

[1]私は自分の知性が衰えてきているような気がしている。[2]この数年間，私は誰か，もしくは何かが私の脳の働き方を変えているという落ち着かない気分がしている。[3]完全に知性を失ったわけではないが，知性が変わりつつあるのが感じとれるのだ。[4]それを最も強く感じるのは，文章を読んでいるときだ。[5]以前は本や長い記事に没頭するのは私には簡単だったが，もはやそんなことはまれにしかない。[6]今では，私の集中力は1，2ページ読んだだけでさまよい始める。[7]私は少し読むと，何か他にやることを探し始める。[8]常に自分の怠惰な脳を文章に引き戻そうとしているような気がするのだ。

1 lose *one's* mind は，ここでは「知性を失う」という文字通りの意味であり，「発狂する，頭がおかしくなる」というイディオムとして使われてはいない。

□ feel like S V ...「まるで…のように感じる」（＝feel as if S V）

2 that 以下は an uncomfortable feeling と同格の名詞節。

□ over A「A（期間）にわたって」　□ the last A「このA（期間），過去A（期間）」

□ uncomfortable「落ち着かない，不安な」　□ the way S V「…する方法，…の仕方」

□ brain「脳」

3 □ not completely「完全に…というわけでない」

6 □ concentration「集中力」　□ start to *do*「…し始める」　□ drift「漂う，さまよう」

7 to do は，something else を修飾する形容詞用法の不定詞句。

□ a little bit「少し」　□ start *doing*「…し始める」　□ look for A「Aを探す」

8 □ pull A back to B「AをBに引き戻す」　□ lazy「怠惰な」　□ text「文章」

第2段落

[1]I think I know what's going on. [2]For well over two decades now, I've been spending a lot of time online, searching and surfing the internet. [3]I'm a writer, so the internet saves me a lot of time when I'm doing research. [4]I use my computer to pay bills, schedule appointments, book flights and hotel rooms, and do many other tasks. [5]Even when I'm not working, I'm reading and writing emails, scanning headlines, flicking through Instagram, watching short videos on YouTube, or just jumping from link to link.

[1]私は何が起きているのかがわかっていると思う。[2]もう20年を優に超える間，私はインターネットで検索をしたりあちこち見て回ったりしながら，オンラインでたくさんの時間を過ごし

てきている。[3]私は著述家なので，調べ物をしているときはインターネットのおかげでたくさんの時間を節約している。[4]私がコンピュータを使うのは，請求書の支払いをしたり，人と会う予定を調整したり，飛行機の便やホテルの部屋を予約したり，その他多くの作業をしたりするためである。[5]仕事をしていないときでも，Eメールを読んだり書いたり，見出しを流し読みしたり，インスタグラムに目を通したり，ユーチューブで短い動画を見たり，ただリンクを次々と飛び回ったりしている。

1 □ go on「起きる，生じる」(＝happen / occur)

2 searching 以下は付帯状況を表す分詞構文。and は searching と surfing の2つの現在分詞を結んでいる。

□ well「(時・場所を表す副詞の前で)はるかに，優に」

□ over A「A(数詞)を超えて，Aより多く」

□ spend「を過ごす，費やす」　□ online「オンラインで，ネット上で」

□ search the internet「インターネットで検索を行う」

□ surf the internet「インターネットのウェブサイトを見て回る」

3 □ writer「著述家，物書き」　□ do research「調査[研究]を行う」

4 to pay 以下は，use my computer を修飾する，目的を表す副詞用法の不定詞句。1つめの and は flights と hotel rooms の2つの名詞(句)を結んでいる。2つめの and は pay bills, schedule appointments, book ... rooms, do ... tasks の4つの動詞句を結んでいる。

□ bill「請求書」　□ schedule「の予定を組む」

□ appointment「(面会の)約束／(医院・美容院などの)予約」　□ book「を予約する」

□ flight「(飛行機の)便」　□ task「作業，仕事」

5 and は reading と writing の2つの現在分詞を結んでいる。or は，reading and writing emails, scanning headlines, flicking through Instagram, watching short videos on YouTube, just jumping from link to link の5つの現在分詞句を結んでいる。

□ scan「を(情報を探して)ざっと読む」　□ headline「(記事の)見出し」

□ flick through A「A(本のページやネットのサイトなど)にざっと目を通す」

□ from A to A「次々にAを，Aを次から次へと」

第3段落

[1]These are all advantages, both for work and play. [2]Such easy access to information! [3]But these advantages come at a price. [4]The internet is not only a channel of information. [5]It also shapes our thought processes. [6]And what the internet seems to be doing is reducing my ability to concentrate and think. [7]Whether I'm online or not, my mind now expects to take in information the way the internet sends it to me: in a fast-moving stream of tiny

information packets. [8]My calm, focused mind is being pushed aside by a new kind of mind that wants to take in information in short, unrelated, and overlapping bursts — the faster the better.

[1]これらはすべて，仕事と遊びの両方にとって利点である。[2]こんなにも簡単な情報へのアクセス！ [3]しかし，これらの利点は大きな代償を伴っている。[4]インターネットは情報の1つのチャンネルであるばかりではない。[5]私たちの思考の過程を形成してもいるのである。[6]そして，インターネットがやっているように思えるのは，私の集中力と思考力を低下させることである。[7]私がネットを使っていてもいなくても，私の知性は，今やインターネットが私に送ってくる通りに，つまり，高速で動く小さな情報のパケットの流れとして，情報を取り入れることを期待しているのである。[8]私の冷静で集中力のある知性は，短くて，関連のない，重複した情報の噴出を取り入れたがっている新しい種類の知性によって押しのけられつつある。速ければ速いほどよいのである。

1 □ advantage for A「Aにとっての利点」　□ both A and B「AとBの両方」

2 名詞句だけで書かれている感嘆文。

□ such (a)＋形容詞＋A「こんなに…なA」

□ access to A「Aへのアクセス，接続」

4 not only X but also Y「XだけでなくYも」の前半に相当する文で，次の第5文が後半に相当する。

5 □ shape「を形作る，形成する」　□ thought process「思考の過程」

6 what the internet seems to be doing が主語となる名詞節で，reducing 以下は補語となる動名詞句。1つめの And は第5文と第6文を結んでいる。2つめの and は concentrate と think の2つの動詞を結んでいる。

□ seem to *do*「…するように思われる」　□ reduce「を弱める，低下させる」

□ ability to *do*「…する能力」　□ concentrate「集中する」

7 □ whether ... or ～「…であろうと～であろうと」　□ expect to *do*「…することを期待する」

□ take A in「Aを取り入れる，吸収する」　□ the way S V「…するように」

□ fast-moving「高速で動く」　□ stream「(情報の)流れ，データストリーム」

□ tiny「小さな」

□ packet「パケット」インターネットで送る情報を小さく分けた単位。

8 be being *done* は進行形の受動態で「…されつつある，…されているところだ」という意味。and は short, unrelated, overlapping という3つの形容詞を結んでいる。

□ calm「冷静な，落ち着いた」　□ focused「集中力のある，集中した」

☐ push A aside「Aを脇に押しのける／Aに取って代わる」

☐ unrelated「関連しない，関係のない」　☐ overlapping「重複している」

☐ burst「爆発，噴出」

☐ the 比較級 ..., the 比較級 ～「…すればするほど，ますます～」

第4段落

[1]Recently, a research company published a study of the effects of internet use on young people. [2]The company interviewed 6,000 college students who have grown up using the internet and reported that the internet has affected the way the young people absorb information. [3]"They don't necessarily read a page from left to right and from top to bottom. [4]They might instead skip around, scanning for important information of interest."

[1]最近，ある調査会社がインターネットの使用が若者に与える影響に関する研究を発表した。[2]その会社は，インターネットを使いながら育った6,000人の大学生にインタビューを行い，インターネットは若者たちが情報を吸収する方法に影響を与えてきている，と報告した。[3]「若者たちは，必ずしもページを左から右へ，そして上から下へ読んではいない。[4]そうではなくて，飛ばし読みをして，興味のある重要な情報のみを拾っているのかもしれない。」

1 ☐ recently「最近」　☐ the effect of A on B「AのBへの影響」

2 who have ... the internet は 6,000 college students を修飾する関係代名詞節。

☐ grow up *doing*「…しながら成長する」　☐ report that 節「…だと報告する」

3 ☐ not necessarily ...「必ずしも…ではない」

4 scanning 以下は付帯状況を表す分詞構文。

☐ instead「そうではなくて，その代わりに」

☐ skip around「飛ばし読みをする，飛び飛びに読む」

☐ scan for A「Aを探してざっと読む」　☐ of interest「面白い，興味深い」(＝interesting)

第5段落

[1]We humans used to have a 'linear' mind—a mind that was good at processing long, difficult text, without losing concentration. [2]But now, that's changing. [3]For the last five centuries, ever since the printing press made book reading a popular activity, the linear mind has been the center of art, science, and society. [4]Now, that mind may be a thing of the past.

[1]私たち人間は，かつては「直線的な」知性，つまり長くて難しい文章を集中力を失わずに処理するのが上手な知性を持っていた。[2]しかし今，それが変わりつつある。[3]過去5世紀の間，印刷機が本を読むことを一般的な活動にして以来ずっと，直線的な知性は芸術，科学，社会の中心であった。[4]今，その知性は過去のものとなっているのかもしれない。

1 We と humans は同格の関係。また，ダッシュ以下は直前の a 'linear' mind を補足説明している。

□ humans「人間」　□ linear「直線的な」

□ be good at *doing*「…するのが上手である，得意である」　□ process「を処理する」

□ without *doing*「…せずに，…することなく」

3 ever since 節内は，the printing press(S) made(V) book reading(O) a popular activity(C)という構造になっている。and は art，science，society の3つの名詞を結んでいる。

□ century「世紀」　□ ever since S V ...「…して以来ずっと」

□ printing press「印刷機」　□ make O C「OをCにする」

□ book reading「本を読むこと，読書」　□ popular「一般的な，一般の人が行う」

□ the center of A「Aの中心」

20 言語の持つ制約

解答

問1　1．現象を記述する。2．現象を評価する。

問2　我々が何かをあるいは誰かを記述しようとするときには，我々が用いる言葉は，自分自身の好き嫌いを反映するという点で，必ずといってよいほど価値観を伴うのである。

問3　イ

問4　Incredible as it may seem

問5　エ．mutual

問6　other people

▶▶▶ 設問解説 ◀◀◀

問1　下線部(1)は「言語は多くの機能を果たしている」という意味。直後の第1段落第2文に「言語の目的の1つは現象を記述する(のを助ける)こと」とあり，第3文に「もう1つの目的は現象を評価すること」とあるので，この2つを答えればよい。

□ serve「を果たす，に役立つ」　□ function「機能」

問2　When we ... or someone と in that ... and dislikes がともに主節を修飾している。in that S V ... は「…するという点で」という意味。なお，we use は the words を修飾する関係代名詞節。

例　I've been lucky in that I have never had to worry about money.
「私は，お金について心配しなければならないことがなかったという点で，恵まれていた」

□ attempt to *do*「…しようとする／…しようという試み」

□ describe「(を)記述する，(の)特徴を述べる」　□ values「価値観」

□ reflect「を反映する」　□ likes and dislikes「好き嫌い」

問3　下線部(3)の直後の文の内容「人を記述するとなると，評価的意味を欠いた言葉を見つけることはほとんど不可能である」から判断する。

問4　接続詞の as は，形容詞＋as S V ... という語順で用いると「…だけれども」という譲歩の意味を表す。ここでは，as it may seem incredible と並べると「…なので」という理由を表すので，we simply ... 以下と意味がつながらない。

例 Unlikely as it may seem, he won the race.

「ありえないと思えるかもしれないけど，彼がそのレースに勝ったのです」

□ incredible「信じられない」　□ seem C「Cのようである」

問5 次の文が that is「すなわち，つまり」で始まっているので，その文と同じ内容になるように，空所(5)に入るものを考える。次の文では「考え方と言語の使い方が相互に影響を与えている」と述べられている。なお，not only X but (also) Y「XだけでなくYも」の not only が S V の前に置かれたことで，倒置が起きていることに注意。

ア.「間接的な」イ.「限られた」ウ.「文化的な」エ.「相互の」

問6 下線部(6)を含む部分の構造は，the words they use(S) tell(V) us(O_1) much (O_2) であり，about them と about the events 以下が比較された同等比較の文。they use は the words を修飾する関係代名詞節で，they は other people を指している。本文では，「記述だけに使われる客観的な言葉はなく，言葉はそれを使う人の価値判断を表す評価的意味を伴う」ことが繰り返し述べられていることから，「他者が使う言葉が，彼らが記述しようとしている出来事や人についてと同じくらい教えてくれる」のは，「言葉を使う人」である。したがって，正解は other people。

Advice 論説文　主題－展開－結論型

論説文では，ある主題をめぐって論を展開した上で，筆者の主張や結論が最後に述べられるという論旨展開をとることがある。特に筆者の個人的な見解や主張などを述べた文章ではこの展開をとることが多い。本問では，第1段落で「記述と評価という言語の2つの機能」が導入として述べられ，第2段落第1文では逆接のディスコース・マーカー But に続いて，疑問文という形で「その2つの機能の不可分性」という主題が提示されている。それ以降でこの問題をめぐって論が展開し，最終段落で「言語の使用に内在する価値判断に注意する必要がある」という結論が述べられている。

要　約

言語は記述と評価を行うが，特に人を記述する際は評価的意味を欠く言葉がないため，中立を保つことができない。考え方と言葉の使い方は相互に影響を及ぼすため，言語の使用に内在する価値判断に注意する必要がある。(100字)

構文・語句解説

第1段落

[1]Language serves many functions. [2]Certainly one of its most common and most important purposes is to help us describe various phenomena, such as events, situations, and people: "What is it?" [3]Another purpose is to evaluate these same phenomena: "Is it good or bad?" [4]Typically, we consider descriptions to be objective, whereas we consider evaluations to be subjective.

[1]言語は多くの機能を果たしている。[2]間違いなく，最も一般的で最も重要な目的の１つは，我々が出来事や状況や人のような様々な現象を記述する，つまり「それは何なのか」ということを記述するのを助けることである。[3]もう１つの目的は，これらの同じ現象を評価する，つまり「それは良いのか悪いのか」と評価することである。[4]概して我々は，記述を客観的であると考える一方で，評価を主観的であると考える。

2 □ certainly「間違いなく，確かに」　□ help O *do*「Oが…するのを助ける」
□ phenomena＜phenomenon「現象」の複数形。　□ situation「状況」
3 □ evaluate「(を)評価する」
4 □ typically「概して／典型的に」　□ description「記述」　□ objective「客観的な」
□ whereas S V ...「ところが一方で…」　□ evaluation「評価」　□ subjective「主観的な」

第2段落

[1]But is the distinction between objective description and subjective evaluation a clear one? [2]The answer, in the vast majority of cases, is no. [3]Why? [4]Because words both describe and evaluate. [5]When we attempt to describe something or someone, the words we use almost always carry values, in that they reflect our own personal likes and dislikes. [6]Thus, our use of any particular term serves not only to describe, but also to assert what is desirable or undesirable to us.

[1]しかし，客観的な記述と主観的な評価の間の区別ははっきりしたものなのだろうか。[2]答えは，大多数の場合，否である。[3]なぜなのだろう。[4]なぜなら，言葉は記述も評価もするからである。[5]我々が何かをあるいは誰かを記述しようとするときには，我々が用いる言葉は，自分自身の好き嫌いを反映するという点で，必ずといってよいほど価値観を伴うのである。[6]したがって，どのような特定の言葉を用いても，記述するだけでなく，我々にとって望ましいこと，あ

るいは望ましくないことを主張することにもなる。

1 □ distinction between A and B「AとBの区別」

2 □ the vast majority of A「Aの大多数」

3 Why? = Why is the answer no?

6 □ any A「〈肯定文で〉どんなAでも」　□ term「言葉」

□ serve to *do*「…するのに役立つ」　□ assert「を主張する」　□ desirable「望ましい」

第3段落

[1]This problem is not so prevalent in the physical sciences, as compared to the social sciences. [2]Let's take, as an illustration, the terms cold and hot. [3]In the field of physical sciences, both terms refer, in a relatively neutral sense, to the rate of molecular vibrations (or temperature): "That liquid is very cold," or "That liquid is very hot." [4]When we use these same terms to describe an individual, however, they take on a distinctly evaluative meaning: "That person is very cold," or "That person is very hot."

[1]この問題は，社会科学と比べて，自然科学の場合にはそれほど広く認められない。[2]例として，「冷たい」「熱い」という言葉を取り上げてみよう。[3]自然科学の分野では，いずれの言葉も，比較的中立的な意味合いで，分子の振動の割合（つまり温度）を表す。すなわち，「あの液体はとても冷たい」とか「あの液体はとても熱い」といった具合である。[4]しかし，これらの同じ言葉をある個人を記述するのに用いると，はっきりとした評価的意味を帯びる。「あの人はとても冷たい」とか「あの人はとても熱い」といった具合になる。

1 □ prevalent「広く認められる，広く行き渡っている」　□ physical science「自然科学」

□ as compared to A「Aと比べて」　□ social science「社会科学」

2 □ illustration「例」

3 □ refer to A「Aを表す，Aに言及する」　□ relatively「比較的」　□ neutral「中立的な」

□ rate「割合」　□ vibration「振動」　□ liquid「液体」

4 □ take on A「A〈様相・性質など〉を帯びる」　□ distinctly「はっきりと」

□ evaluative「評価的な」

第４段落

[1]What are the consequences of the evaluative bias of language? [2]The words that we use can, with or without intention, become powerful instruments of change. [3]In those instances where we are deliberately attempting to influence others to agree with our point of view, we intentionally select words that most persuasively communicate our values. [4]In many cases, however, the process is unintentional. [5]Our best attempts to remain neutral are restricted by the limits of language. [6]When it comes to describing people it is nearly impossible to find words that are empty of evaluative meaning. [7]Incredible as it may seem, we simply don't have neutral adjectives to describe personality characteristics. [8]And even if such words did exist, we still would be very likely to utilize the ones that reflect our own personal preferences.

[1]言語が持つ評価的偏りの結果はどうなるのであろう。[2]我々が用いる言葉は，意図しようとしまいと，変化をもたらすための強力な道具となりえる。[3]他者に自分の考えに同意してもらおうと計画的に働きかける場合には，我々は最も説得力を持って自分の価値観を伝える言葉を意図的に選択する。[4]しかし，多くの場合，その過程は意図的なものではない。[5]中立を保とうと最善を尽くしてみても，言語の限界によって制限されてしまう。[6]人を記述するとなると，評価的意味を欠いた言葉を見つけることはほとんど不可能である。[7]信じられないと思えるかもしれないが，人格的特徴を記述する中立的な形容詞はまったくないのだ。[8]それに，もし仮にそのような言葉が存在するとしても，我々はなお自分自身の個人的好みを反映する言葉を使ってしまう可能性がきわめて高い。

1 □ consequence「結果」　□ bias「偏り」

2 □ intention「意図」　□ instrument「道具」

3 where we ... of view は those instances を修飾する関係副詞節。

□ instance「場合／例」　□ deliberately「計画的に，故意に」

□ influence O to *do*「Oに…するように働きかける」　□ agree with A「Aに同意する」

□ point of view「観点」　□ intentionally「意図的に」　□ persuasively「説得力を持って」

5 □ remain C「Cのままである」　□ restrict「を制限する」

6 □ when it comes to A「Aということになると」　□ be empty of A「Aを欠いている」

7 □ simply not「まったく…でない」　□ adjective「形容詞」　□ personality「人格，個性」

□ characteristic「特徴」

8 even if such words did exist, we still would be ... は仮定法過去。did は動詞強調の助動詞。ones は words の代用。

□ be likely to *do*「…する可能性がある，たぶん…するだろう」　□ utilize「を用いる」
□ preference「好み」

第5段落

[1]This also emphasizes the mutual influence of attitudes and language. [2]That is, not only do our attitudes and perceptions affect our use of language, but our use of language in turn influences our attitudes and perceptions.

[1]このことはまた，考え方と言語が相互に影響を及ぼすことを強調している。[2]すなわち，我々の考え方と認識が言語の使い方に影響するだけでなく，同様に言語の使い方が考え方や認識に影響を及ぼすのである。

1 □ emphasize「を強調する」　□ attitude「考え方，態度」
2 □ perception「認識」　□ in turn「今度は，次に」

第6段落

[1]Because of the evaluative bias of language, we must be careful both to become aware of our own personal values and to communicate these values as openly and fairly as possible. [2]In other words, we should avoid presenting our value judgments as objective reflections of truth. [3]We should also be alert to the value judgments inherent in other people's use of language, and in many cases the words they use tell us at least as much about them as about the events and individuals they are attempting to describe.

[1]言語が持つ評価的偏りのために，我々は自分自身の個人的な価値観を意識し，こうした価値観をできる限り率直に公正に伝えるように注意しなければならない。[2]言い換えれば，我々は自分の価値判断を真実を客観的に反映するものとして示すことを避けるようにすべきである。[3]また，我々は他者の言葉の使い方に内在する価値判断に注意しなければならず，多くの場合彼らが使う言葉は，彼らが記述しようとしている出来事や人についてと少なくとも同じくらい彼ら自身についても教えてくれるのである。

1 □ be careful to *do*「…するように気をつける」　□ as ... as possible「できる限り…」
□ openly「率直に，公然と」
2 □ in other words「言い換えれば」　□ present「を示す」　□ reflection「反映」

3 inherent in other people's use of language は the value judgments を修飾する形容詞句。they are attempting to describe は the events and individuals を修飾する関係代名詞節。

□ be alert to A「Aに用心する」　□ inherent in A「Aに内在する，固有の」